P9-DFC-470

When People Care Enough To Act

Mike Green
with
Henry Moore & John O'Brien

Foreword by
John L. McKnight

Reflections by

Dan Duncan, Jan Fitzgerald , Mike Mather, Beth Mount,
Terry Pickett, Ted Smeaton , & Christine Soto

INCLUSION PRESS

A Note On Authorship

This book is the result of two collaborations. Mike Green and Henry Moore developed the approach to doing and teaching ABCD organizing that forms the basis of the book. Mike Green and John O'Brien collaborated in writing the book, which reflects Mike's learning about ABCD organizing. Except in contributions signed by someone else, Mike is the "I" in the book's first person statements.

An Inclusion Press Book
Published by Inclusion Press

Copyright© 2006 Inclusion Press
Second Printing October 2008

Printed in Canada by Couto Prnting & Publishing

Printed on stock containing post consumer recycled content

Library and Archives Canada Cataloguing in Publication

Green, Mike, 1947-   When people care enough to act : ABCD in action / Mike Green with Henry Moore & John O'Brien ; foreword by John McKnight ; reflections by Dan Duncan ... [et al.].

Includes bibliographical references and index.   ISBN-13: 978-1-895418-74-3

ISBN-10: 1-895418-74-7

1. Community development. 2. Community organization--Citizen participation. 3. Communication in community development. I. Moore, Henry, 1949- II. O'Brien, John, 1946- III. Title.

HN49.C6G735 2006   361.2'5   C2006-904652-2

Preparation of this publication was partially supported through a subcontract to Responsive Systems Associates from the Center on Human Policy, Syracuse University for the Research and Training Center on Community Living. The Research and Training Center on Community Living is supported through a cooperative agreement (number H133B031116) between the National Institute on Disability & Rehabilitation Research (NIDRR) and the University of Minnesota Institute on Community Integration. Members of the Center are encouraged to express their opinions; these do not necessarily represent the official position of NIDRR.

47 Indian Trail   tel. 416.658.5363   info@inclusion.com
Toronto, ON   M6R 1Z8   fax. 416.658.5067   **inclusion.com**

Contents

Exercises to Strengthen Community Building

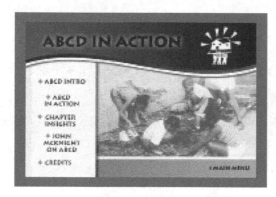

In the companion DVD, ABCD in Action, you can visit five communities that have put the lessons in this book into action, see and hear Henry Moore and Mike Green present the key ideas in this book, and learn about the foundations of ABCD from John McKnight. Visit www.inclusion.com for more information.

DVD Table of Contents

Acknowledgements

We want to thank John McKnight who has been our guide to ABCD and our friend for over fifteen years. The ideas in this book were shaped by our experiences with many people: Jody Kretzmann, the ABCD Institute faculty circle of friends, and the people we have met who are seeking practical ways to to make things better in their home communities by applying the ABCD approach on "Monday morning".

We have often talked about how we do this work for our two daughters: Henry's daughter Morgan and Mike's daughter Annie. We want so much that they know a community life that is truly good. Each of our daughters has known discrimination: Morgan from racism as an African-American young woman, and Annie from being labeled disabled. We are both now in our later fifties and can see ahead to our lives ending. This makes us both very much aware of the importance of contributing to the emergence of young leaders like our daughters. Time is short and people matter most.

Ten years ago Judith Snow said to Mike, "you have a book inside you ready to write." Three years ago Jan Fitzgerald said, "You have something to say." Two years ago, at the first Minnowbrook Inclusion Conference sponsored by the Adirondack ARC, Jack Pearpoint and John O'Brien said, "We will help you write a book and produce a DVD about your work with Henry" This book would not have happened without the collaboration of Mike and Henry to define the ideas. But Jack urged us on to really believe we could do it, and John O'Brien became the book's conductor, with deep listening, insightful choreography, and constant encouragement as Mike struggled to write the book's text over the past two years.

Finally, we acknowledge that in every local community ordinary people act with great courage, love and commitment to create a world where human beings can live a truly human life. We draw inspiration and knowledge from their work.

– Mike Green and Henry Moore

Foreword

This is a book by two of North America's master practitioners of Asset-Based Community Development –Mike Green and Henry Moore. Their work has advanced the field of Asset Based Community Development by focusing on the fact that citizens are the primary asset and activators of assets in local communities.

Citizens are, of course, the producers of democracy. And strong local communities are created when citizens are also the producers of the future. They cannot be replaced. No professional, institution, business or government can substitute for the power, creativity or relevance of productive local citizens. That is why Asset Based Community Development is, in practice, citizen centered community building.

This citizen-centered guide is the work of two great citizens. Mike Green has experience as a businessman, social worker, community organizer and Asset Based practitioner. He has combined all this practice in unique Asset-Based approaches to local organizing and inclusion of people who live at the margins.

Henry Moore's inventiveness as a city official has taught institutional leaders across North America how to **lead by stepping back**. He has shown how to support and nourish local citizen action rather than control, stifle or dominate local citizen efforts.

In this book, Mike Green and Henry Moore point the way toward creating a powerful citizen-centered local democracy that solves problems, welcomes all neighbors and creates a community of genuine care. Following their path will also lead to the discovery of our personal capacity to renew our own lives by connecting ourselves to the riches that surround us. We are, after all, not people half full. We are a people whose cup runs over.

Because Mike and Henry see this so clearly, they are wonderful guides to rediscovering the assets that we can use as we grow powerful as citizens, and our democracy comes alive again.

–John L. McKnight

Co-Director, Asset Based Community Development Institute

Northwestern University. Evanston, IL

When people discover what they have, they find power.

When people join together in new connections and relationships they build power.

When people become more productive together, they exercise their power to address problems and realize dreams.

1

Community Partnerships That Work

From Helping Communities to Helping Communities Help Themselves

Our local communities have many serious problems. How do people leave poverty? What do we do about violence? How do we help our young people find a good future? What can we do to increase literacy? How do we make our communities safe and healthy? What do we do about drug abuse? What about housing homeless people? How can people with disabilities become real community members? How do we develop our local economy and create new jobs?

In North America, as in many places, professional helpers have the principal responsibility, power, and control of resources for community problem solving. We expect teachers to educate our children, doctors to heal us, the police to make us safe, human services to help us, public health organizations to protect us, city government to develop strong neighborhoods, development agencies to create jobs, and on and on. When problems arise in communities, we tend to see helping agencies with their programs and services as the solution. But, increasingly, helping agencies are overextended, without adequate resources to address the problems they face. The limited results of over-stretched professional help disturb investors of both public taxpayer money and private foundation money. Awareness of the need for a new approach grows. More and more agency leaders, researchers, and policy planners recognize that social and economic problems can only be addressed effectively by involving a larger part of the *whole* community.

Many community problems can only be addressed if a wider partnership of local people work together. Schools cannot succeed by the efforts of teachers and administrators alone, but only when parents, students, and neighbors work with them. City government cannot create safe communities unless police, city officials, and neighborhood groups all work together. People can best leave poverty when local businesses, human services, residents, and congregations create partnerships that build a bridge to real economic opportunities. Human services can't help people with disabilities unless residents, local associations, and businesses welcome people with disabilities as real members of their communities. Public health agencies cannot address AIDS without common effort that includes schools, congregations, residents, and local agencies. Youth have the best job prospects when they are productively connected to their community's adults.

In every segment of community life there is a new understanding: when a growing circle of people work together in community partnership, they have the power to address important problems and to achieve the goals they want. Strong communities know that they need everyone to give their gifts if the community is to thrive. It is true: there is no one we don't need.

Asset Based Community Development

We may have all come on different ships,
but we are in the same boat now.
—Dr. Martin Luther King

How does a community develop a wider circle of people working together to address important problems and realize ambitious goals? **Asset Based Community Development (ABCD)** is a powerful approach focused on discovering and mobilizing the resources that are *already present* in a community. The ABCD point of view encourages people to recognize that their community is a glass half full of assets, not a glass half empty with needs. Community assets are resources that become valuable when they are brought together and made productive. The ABCD approach provides a way for citizens to find and mobilize what they have in order to build a stronger community.

John McKnight, whose research with Jody Kretzmann defined the ABCD approach, once said, "ABCD is like a closet organizer to make sense of the messiness of community life." After listening to many different stories of successful community building over many years, Jody and John asked themselves what was common to all these unique stories. It was like they had asked people about their favorite cake, heard a thousand different recipes, and then asked themselves, "What do all those cakes have in common, whether chocolate, carrot, or lemon?" In the case of cakes, the four most common ingredients are flour, eggs, sugar, and butter. In the case of successful community building, there are three fundamental qualities of development efforts that successfully connect and mobilize the building blocks of community.

Effective community development has three qualities. It is asset based, internally focused, and relationship driven. **Asset based** means that the focus is on discovering what can be productive in a community. What do we already have that will allow us to do something worthwhile? **Internally focused** recognizes that the best starting place is what can be found inside a community. The people who live in a community are the key contributors to community development that works. **Relationship driven** reminds us that communities only get strong through connections among people that permit people to give their gifts. Relationship building is the fundamental action of community building.

Asset based

Internally focused

Relationship driven

Relationships reveal a community's assets and the possibilities for generating productive connections among the five building blocks of community. These building blocks are...

- **Individuals** with gifts, talents, and skills to contribute. People's gifts are the most fundamental building block of community. Every person has many gifts to contribute if given the invitation and the opportunity.

- **Local voluntary associations** in which groups of people act together out of care; for example: neighborhood groups, congregations, self-help groups, fraternal organizations, choirs, book clubs, garden clubs.

- **Institutions** of business, government, and nonprofit organizations: for example, local businesses, parks, libraries, schools, hospitals, nonprofit agencies, churches, and religious institutions. Every institution can support local individuals and their associations.

- **The local economy.** Economic exchange circulates money, goods, and services through a community as people buy, sell, hire, and invest.

- **The physical world**, both natural and constructed: rivers, landscapes, buildings, fields, streets, and the transportation infrastructure.

The hard truth is that development must start from within the community and, in most of our urban neighborhoods, there is no other choice. Creative neighborhood leaders across the country have begun to recognize this hard truth, and have shifted their practices accordingly. They are discovering that wherever there are effective community development efforts, those efforts are based upon an understanding, or map, of the community's assets, capacities and abilities. For it is clear that even the poorest neighborhood is a place where individuals and organizations represent resources upon which to rebuild. The key to neighborhood regeneration, then, is to locate all of the available local assets, to begin connecting them with one another in ways that multiply their power and effectiveness, and to begin harnessing those local institutions that are not yet available for local development purposes.

This entire process begins with the construction of a new 'map.' Once this guide to capacities has replaced the old one containing only needs and deficiencies, the regenerating community can begin to assemble its strengths into new combinations, new structures of opportunity, new sources of income and control, and new possibilities for production.

...it is clear that the strong ties which form the basis for community-based problem solving have been under attack. The forces driving people apart are many and frequently cited.... Because of these factors, the sense of efficacy based on interdependence, the idea that people can count on their neighbors and neighborhood resources for support and strength has weakened. For community builders who are focused on assets, rebuilding these local relationships offers the most promising route toward successful community development.

–Jody Kretzmann and John McKnight,
Building Communities from the Inside Out

For a summary of John McKnight's thinking, turn to page 160.

John McKnight   Jody Kretzmann

ABCD makes visible and concrete the basic structure for building a strong community. Strength comes from three interconnected activities: **discovering** local assets, **connecting** these assets to work together, and then **creating opportunities** for these assets to be productive and powerful together. When a group of people discover what they have, they find power. When people join together in new connections and relationships, they build power. When people become more productive together, they exercise their power to address problems and realize dreams. Together we are better.

What to Do on Monday Morning?

Six years ago Henry Moore and I led a five-day workshop on Asset Based Community Development (ABCD) in the New Mexico mountains. On the fifth morning a pediatrician from Ohio said, "I love ABCD, but I have one question. What on earth do I actually do on Monday morning?" We realized that this was our question, the question that guides our work. Since the doctor from Ohio challenged us to be relevant to his Monday morning, Henry and I have worked to create learning structures for people who love the ABCD perspective and need some help to work out how to act on ABCD in practical ways. We apply and refine these structures through consultation with community leaders and in workshops, and now in this book and its companion DVD.

Our approach builds on a foundation of proven community organizing principles, principles that guide collective action on issues that people care enough to act on. One distinctive feature of our work is our focus on discovering ways that governments and service agencies can effectively engage their commu-

Henry Moore   Mike Green

nities as partners to strengthen citizens. Our *ABCD Training Group*, which is associated with *The ABCD Institute* of Jody Kretzmann and John McKnight, links Henry's long experience in transforming city government to support citizens with my experience in community organizing and social work to connect citizens for action. Our aim is to produce practical ways to energize growing circles of community groups to work together in partnership and make their communities stronger, safer, healthier, and more productive. Three key themes define our framework for action:

- Assets focus
- Applying community organizing principles
- Agencies that lead by stepping back

Assets: There is More There Than Anyone Knows

Practical action starts with the understanding that every community has more potential resources than any one person knows. Your community has a wide variety of assets that can be identified, connected, and made productive, if you find these resources and organize them to work together for the benefit of the community. There are residents, local associations, congregations, businesses, nonprofit agencies, and government agencies. Seeing all the assets of a community is like looking through a kaleidoscope: many colored chips of glass fit together in many different ways as you turn the scope. Community assets fit together in many different and unexpected ways to create new possibilities. The presence of hidden assets and unrealized connections means that communities can have very serious problems and still have capacity to join in solving them.

There is an old saying, "The difference between heaven and hell is just a new pair of glasses". You find what you are looking for: emptiness or capacity. This workbook uses ABCD's lenses as a way to discover community resources and then to develop actions that use and strengthen them.

Community Organizing: Connecting Groups of People to Act on What They Care About

Care is woven throughout all the groups in any community. There are people in every part of every community who care enough to act on issues that matter to their common life. What people care about enough to do something about is the key asset in every community. As what people care about becomes audible and visible, a widening circle of people can recognize common ground and unite to take action. Community organizing is a proven way to find care in a community and to develop ways that people can act on what they care about. Ever since the 1940s, when Saul Alinsky worked in poor neighborhoods in Chicago, community organizing has focused on how people can come together to become an engine for developing their community. For community organizing, the center of development work is the agenda and action of people who live, work, and worship in a community. Community organizing principles are a practical foundation for building successful community partnerships.

Strong People and Effective Programs—It Takes Both

Building strong communities requires both effective helping programs and strong groups of people. An important part of our framework for community development is clarifying and differentiating the best roles for agencies and their programs and the best roles for community groups of people. People and their community groups have to step forward –growing in responsibility, power, and authority– for community problem solving to be successful. Agencies and their programs can offer good services while also helping citizens do what only strong citizens can do: mobilize the wider community to work together. Agencies are more effective when they **lead by stepping back** and offer their agency's assets for citizens to use, find and connect community assets, and support citizens to organize their communities.

Building the Road as You Walk It: Guiding Principles, Not Recipes

How do you get to Carnegie Hall? Practice, practice, practice.
–Old saying among musicians

Each community development group has to find its own unique path to success. There is no one model or recipe. People often want specific formulas, recipes, and models for community development that they can replicate. The desire to build from other's blueprints is understandable, but that approach does not work very well because each situation is unique. Guiding principles about how things work in communities are much more useful than a specific recipe. Principles can help you *decide* what is worth doing in your particular situation. Good community building is an art, not a technology. People learn best how to build community partnership from experience, by having clear principles of practice, and by getting guidance from other successful community builders.

This book offers some basic ideas about what to do and what not to do. These general principles for community partnerships that work —learned from the experience of many people walking on similar roads— can help you stay on the road (and keep out of the ditch at the side of the road) as you construct your own approach.

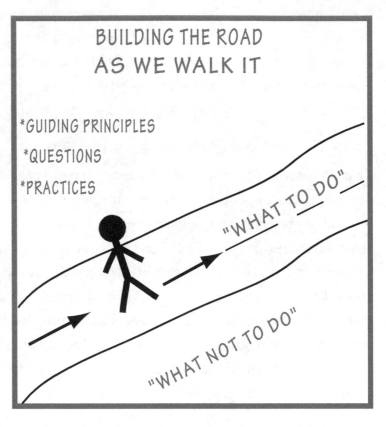

BUILDING THE ROAD AS WE WALK IT

*GUIDING PRINCIPLES
*QUESTIONS
*PRACTICES

"WHAT TO DO"

"WHAT NOT TO DO"

Each chapter in this book builds on the previous chapter's theme and provides a foundation for practical action. Within each chapter is a description of principles of practice, methods, exercises, and questions for discussion. For best results, do not read this book by yourself. Learning about community practice is best done in a group of people who are thinking and talking together.

This book is an effort to bring common sense to how we help communities. You will not find research citations. Instead you will find examples from our personal experience, lessons from the common experience of successful community builders, and references to common sense.

Every person who reads this book can do something to build a stronger community, to make a place where people can act like citizens who care for each other. You may be reading this book as an agency leader, an agency employee, a staff community organizer in a neighborhood, the leader of an association, or as a citizen of your community. Whatever your role, you can take action to build citizenship and strengthen local democracy. The goal of this book is to clarify each reader's options to act more effectively for a stronger community.

Community building is not complex conceptually, but it is often very difficult in practice. I encourage you to do two things. First, use this workbook as a way to clarify your personal framework of practice: your guiding principles and guiding questions about what to do and what not to do. Second, read between the lines and pay attention to what is evoked in you as you read, discuss the ideas, and do the exercises. This workbook is meant to be a friendly catalyst to you, the community builder. I encourage you to examine your heart, your mind, and your experience about your place in your community and how you might move from your present situation toward your dream of a desirable future.

Practical action starts with the understanding that every community has more potential resources than any one person knows.

The Transformation of King Henry

Henry Moore

I recently learned that I have cancer of the lymph nodes. Nevertheless, I am very upbeat. I have a very good chance for a full recovery. My family and my support network are lifting me up, and I am doing everything I ever wanted to do. I am enjoying my family, watching my daughter Morgan (who is now 16 years old) grow up. I really enjoy watching my wife, Donna guide Morgan's development helping her prepare for college and adulthood. My work, which takes me to about 50 cities a year to teach and consult and help people think about how to move institutions to be more productive by engaging citizen leadership, continues to vibrantly fulfill my vision of helping others to build thriving communities.

When I first got my cancer diagnosis, I called a colleague from Baton Rouge to tell her that I didn't think I would be able to finish our work together because I would have to focus on the challenge ahead. She said, "Well, Henry Moore, I hope you don't think you're going to get off that easy. I've had cancer twice and I beat it both times. I took my chemotherapy on Friday and I was back at work on Monday. So I expect you to be here for the job." And I said, "Yes, ma'am."

My ability to do that job —and to benefit from the many relationships and resources and satisfactions my work brings me— is the result of my amazing life journey. I want to tell part of the story of that journey here.

Growing up on a farm in rural North Carolina, where life was difficult, I had this image of helping people and being a help to my community. This vision led me through college and, in 1981, it led me to begin 17 years of service in Savannah, Georgia, as assistant city manager. Under the gold dome of City Hall, I worked hard on the mission of providing services to improve the community. We used management by objectives, problem solving, resource allocation, and timeliness to improve public facilities and services. We won awards that recognized our effectiveness.

Yet we hit a ceiling, especially with the advent of crack cocaine. Citizens acted like consumers of government services, saying "Give me something. I want you to come and fix me, fix where I live, fix this problem." Many citizens did not see themselves as producers of neighborhood well-being. Recognizing this limit brought an important turn in my journey as I learned a difficult and critical lesson: that **we managers must lead by stepping back**. Our success is measured by the extent to which residents take ownership of the mission of neighborhood revitalization. Community leaders must drive community improvement and our task as managers is to develop the skills, the resources, and the relationships to assist them. Managers must also transform organizations to nurture, lift up and support citizens.

My journey's turn toward a new form of leadership began at a workshop with a 90 year old guy named Ed Deming who had been a management improvement pioneer in Japan. He said that transforming any organization means that people in organizations themselves must get stronger, and then they will think of ways to be more productive, making the organization more effective and also benefiting themselves.

The second big step came at the Center for Creative Leadership in Greensboro, North Carolina. Their intensive leadership development session included collecting "360° feedback" from my subordinates. They said, in effect, that I was an SOB, and I learned that people in Savannah called me "King Henry." (My wife Donna said that she could have told me that before the session, saving the City $3,000).

I realized that when I went on vacation my employees went on vacation, and that if I wasn't around nothing was getting done. I had to "transform Henry" in order to be more effective. Top-down management doesn't really work. In effective organizations, the lights are still on when you go home. I recognized that we needed new skills to complement the traditional skills taught in management school. New skills such as listening, nurturing, supporting, asking, and acting on what people say to us.

People must drive community improvement and our task as managers is to develop the skills, the resources, and the relationships to assist them.

I began to figure out how to make the whole organization work better by stepping back. Instead of cultivating employee yes-men, I began to cultivate **gappers**: people from our organization who really cared about working "in the gap" between city government and neighborhood residents to develop new connections and relationships and lift up communities. Instead of simply trying to fix communities, we asked citizens about their priorities. We found that each neighborhood had its own priority: improving housing, or combating drugs and crime, or eradicating blight. We listened to what community residents were saying and we tried to find ways of closing gaps, helping them to lift up their own communities to accelerate revitalization.

Leaders must not be at the top of a pyramid with citizens at the bottom. Leaders must be inside a circle with other partners.

We discovered how to surface new leaders in a community, how to get them involved and how to sustain their involvement over time. One significant step was the creation of "Grants for Blocks", which provided grants of up to $500 for residents to do what ever they wanted to improve their neighborhood, provided that it didn't benefit them personally. They planted flowers, cleaned up vacant lots, established tool banks, and otherwise used the money to make visible improvements in their neighborhoods. People who wanted to contribute their skills, gifts, and capacities came forward in ways that we had not known were possible before we stepped back and offered support. Citizens mobilized and our organization realigned itself to help residents plan and implement neighborhood revitalization.

Most important, we nurtured bottom-up neighborhood leadership. Savannah began to physically improve neighborhoods and to build the trusting relationships with the community that are necessary for sustained improvement. This transformation was difficult and it took time, but it was successful. Active residents came to City Council meetings, zoning hearings, and neighborhood meetings. Residents not only expressed their vision for safe and attractive neighborhoods, they worked together to achieve those visions.

After leaving City Hall, I began to help other communities to apply these lessons. My work focuses on building community partnerships that mobilize citizens. I help people think about how they can build strong organizations that are sensitive to their mission and engaged with their community. I look for ways that residents can gain their own strength, take ownership, and lift up their communities.

Some communities, such as these three, have made remarkable progress.

- **Fremont, California,.** This very diverse city of over 200,000 people speaking many languages, adopted an ordinance for community engagement. The entire city organization made a commitment to increased community involvement. They hired a community organizer and held a community summit with over 500 persons to determine how to improve the community. (See Fremont's tools for neighborhood engagement at www.ci.fremont.ca.us/Community/CommunityInvolvement/default.htm)

- **Staunton, Virginia** (the birthplace of council/manager government), The City Manager hired me to help build a community partnership with an African-American neighborhood that still holds annual reunions for a high school that closed 40 years ago. The association and the Booker T. Washington Community Center became the base for a partnership with the broader community that developed a plan for the neighborhood and for the city as a whole. The neighborhood and the city are making remarkable progress.

- **Seattle, Washington.** Despite budget cuts, the city keeps building community partnerships. A Neighborhood Service Unit, located in the Police Department, represents a bottom-up approach to engage citizens in making the community safer.

Across the nation the statistics are clear: the safest neighborhoods are those in which people know their neighbors, talk to each other, watch each other's houses when they're away, and otherwise ensure that their neighborhoods are safe. This citizen action would be fundamental to safety even if it were possible for the city to provide more and more police officers.

In my journey I have come to fully understand John McKnight's message: institutions must do what cannot be done by citizens, but we must give citizens the space to reclaim their own communities. Leaders must not be at the top of a pyramid with citizens at the bottom. Leaders must be inside a circle with other partners and stakeholders. Our organizations and institutions must step back. In doing this, there are two rules. Rule number one is, citizens have the answers. Rule number two: when in doubt, refer to rule number one.

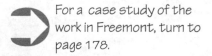

For a case study of the work in Freemont, turn to page 178.

Two Paths -- Two Solutions

Needs	Assets
(What is not there.)	(What is there.)
Services to Meet Needs	Connections & Contributions
Consumers	Citizens
Programs are the answer	People are the answer

II
Finding & Mobilizing Assets In Your Community

Every citizen has gifts. A strong community knows
it needs everyone to give their gifts
–John McKnight

Since 1993, when Jody Kretzmann and John McKnight distilled it's principles in *Building Communities from the Inside Out*, Asset Based Community Development (ABCD) has proven valuable to many people. The ABCD perspective encourages community builders to focus on discovering, connecting, and using the resources within their communities to address their most significant problems and develop their highest potentials. Community builders successfully discover and mobilize assets by creating relationships among people and connections among community groups. Their efforts are based on three principles.

1. Every community has more assets than any one person or group knows.

2. These assets hold the key to sustainable community development and the citizens who can mobilize these assets are at the center of efforts for development.

3. Assets become visible through relationships. These revealing and mobilizing relationships begin in listening for what people care about.

This chapter shows the way to find, connect, and utilize community assets.

Map Assets, Not Needs

ABCD points out a different road to stronger communities than other, more common approaches to community problem solving do. Many common approaches begin by counting up "what is not there," and making a **needs map** to pick out the road to professional problem solving. Professional helpers, from public health and education to human services and public administration, learn the needs assessment and problem solving analysis approach and become expert at making, reading, and responding to needs maps.

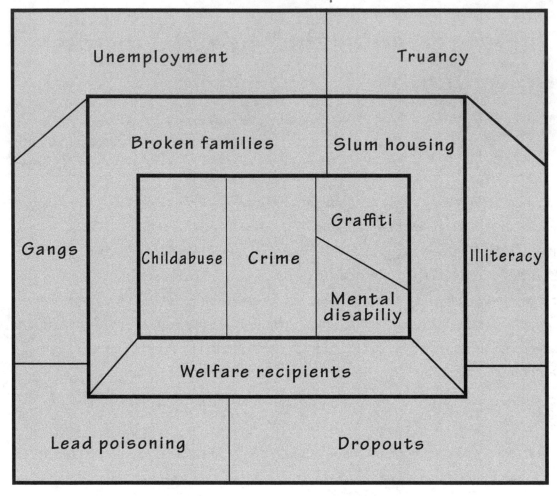

Needs and problems are very real in communities, so the needs map is not an illusion. The problem is that a needs map directs attention away from citizens and their assets and toward experts and their outside remedies for deficiencies. The needs map reinforces the belief that professionally defined and delivered services will best supply what the needs map shows is missing from a community.

Following the needs map mobilizes only a small part of a community's capacity: specifically, the work of professional service providers. Taking the needs map as the starting place for action focuses funds, human and organizational resources, and decision making authority on professionals and service providers. This leaves the knowledge, skills, and resources of citizens on the sidelines, or, at best, in a secondary role. There are at least four disadvantages to the needs map:

- Emphasis on professional helpers as the primary solution undermines citizens' confidence and willingness to invest their talents when they see that those in control of resources act as if only professional outsiders have what it takes to make a difference in their lives.

- The needs map fragments development efforts because it breaks the community up based on professionally determined categories for funding and service delivery.

- People who are good at describing their community as broken often get promoted as leaders by outside helpers. This can weaken more legitimate and positive local leadership.

- Both citizens and service providers often internalize needs map descriptions as negative "truths" about the community. This can make people pessimistic about the possibilities for improvement and discourage them from reaching out to discover what other citizens care about enough to act.

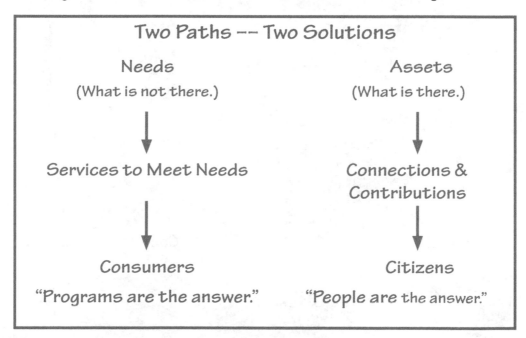

ABCD shows another way to develop communities: the **assets map**. In contrast to the needs map, assets map makers start by counting up "what is there"- identifying what a community already has that can contribute to solving problems and realizing goals. Who and what do we have? What can they do? The next page shows the kinds of assets available in almost any neighborhood.

Community Assets Map

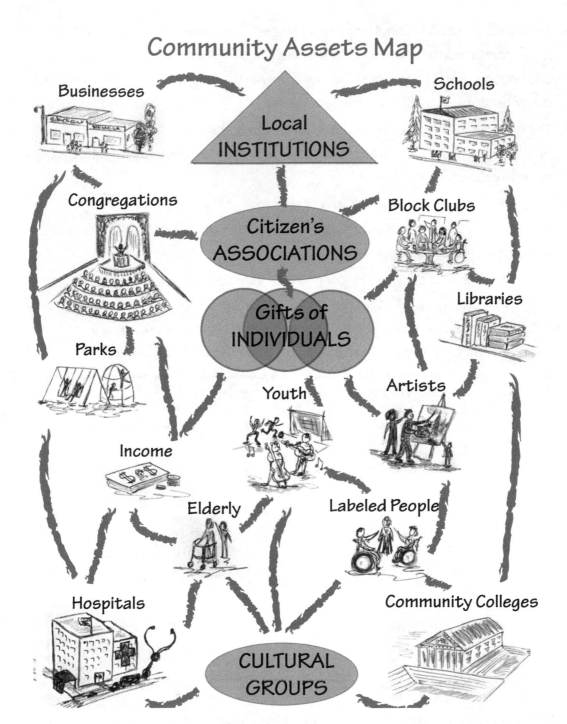

Businesses

Local INSTITUTIONS

Schools

Congregations

Citizen's ASSOCIATIONS

Block Clubs

Gifts of INDIVIDUALS

Libraries

Parks

Youth

Artists

Income

Elderly

Labeled People

Hospitals

CULTURAL GROUPS

Community Colleges

Think about how much capacity in any community could be, but is not engaged in building a better life. Everyone can make a difference. Who can't contribute to a safer healthier community? Almost everyone has gifts to give, contributions to make –if only they are asked and given the opportunity. Look at how neighbors keep sidewalks clean, plant flowers, implement neighborhood watches, form associations, join congregations, start soccer leagues, have block parties, tutor kids in reading, organize resident groups and work together to make a thousand other contributions.

Exercise
You Have More Assets than You Think You Do!

Form groups of three people. Name all the specific assets in your community that can be useful to young people being successful. Who has something to offer young people growing stronger? Make this list together in twenty minutes.

Reflection: Use this space to record what you learned from making this list of assets. What guiding principles or guiding questions does this suggest for your work?

Comment: People are often surprised at how narrow their first idea is about who can be helpful to young people. Professional workers —teachers, police, counselors, social workers, and so forth— come easiest to mind. The truth is that almost everyone has something good to offer towards the success of young people, if only we identify their assets and ask for their contribution.

Discover Assets By Building Relationships

Every community that is getting stronger has at its center an effort to build up a wider circle of people who choose to take action for the common good. There is an old saying among community organizers that "power is in relationships." This is very true. A community is headed toward a better future when people realize that "together we are better" and start building partnerships that reach beyond differences. A strong community is one where action deepens the conviction that everyone has something to contribute and there is no one we don't need. We need each other. You may sell burgers at one end of the street, and I may sell pizza at the other end of the street. We are competitors in supplying meals, but, if we are smart, we work together to make a clean and safe street for everyone.

Keep Citizens At The Center

When communities are doing well, the local residents and their associations and congregations are at the center of development decisions. Often community development has been controlled by outside decision-makers who hold on to the authority to make plans and allocate resources. This "outside-in" approach is usually as ineffective as throwing seeds on concrete. On the other hand, local citizens who believe in and are committed to act on a development agenda can find and till the good soil where seeds can grow into solutions. People who have a problem are most likely to know what to do about it. People inside a community have more motivation to involve others in action and more connections through which to reach them. **Inside-out works**.

Advocates for the ABCD approach generally find agreement with the first two key ideas: having an assets focus and mobilizing local power through relationship building. But citizen-centered development is more challenging because it requires a relocation of responsibility and authority to control resources . It moves power from agencies outside communities to citizens in communities.

Mobilize The Building Blocks of Community

There are five basic building blocks in any community: individuals; associations and congregations; institutions –business, nonprofit agencies, and government agencies; the local economy; and the physical world. Local cultures, ways of communication, community vision and community history form the mortar that holds these building blocks together. **Motivation to act**, what people care about enough to do something about, brings community to life by energizing action around what really matters to citizens. Building a strong community involves finding local assets and connecting them into a wider and wider circle of contribution where assets are productive. To discover and mobilize a community's assets, use each building block as a starting place for building relationships and connecting .

Individuals with Gifts to Contribute

In any community, the most fundamental building block is individual people's capacity to join in contributing their gifts to strengthen their community. Every individual has many gifts –knowledge, skills, and innate talents, gifts of the head, hand, and heart.

A very powerful way to build a stronger community taps unrealized potential in two steps. Ask people, "What are your gifts?" Then connect gifts to opportunities for contribution. When people purposefully look for gifts, there are amazing discoveries. The key is asking. The most fundamental action of community building is conversation, people turning to one another and asking each other what is important to them and what they have to offer to a common effort to work to get what is important.

Gifts of the head – knowledge, information

Gifts of the hand – practical skills

Gifts of the heart – for example, passion, listening

Exercise:

Conversation to Discover Gifts.

Form pairs. Have a twenty-minute one-to-one conversation to discover the other person's gifts. For ten minutes, let one person be the asker while the other person describes his or her gifts. Focus on telling about gifts you enjoy giving in your personal life. Then switch roles.

Reflection: Use this space to record what you learned from listening and talking about gifts. How do the gifts you identified in this conversation connect you to the work of community building?

Comment: People are always surprised at how many gifts each person has. It is also striking how often the energy rises in the room during these conversations. Participants can discover previously unknown gifts and talents in people they have known for many years. This opportunity to find new capacity exists in every work group, neighborhood, association, or congregation. All it takes are conversations in which people inquire about capacities and then listen carefully.

People Whose Gifts Are Invisible. Every community has people who are seen as not having gifts. This mistaken perception has great cost for us all. We waste peoples' gifts, gifts that we need. Strong communities have a **treasure hunt mentality**, in which people look at everyone as bearing gifts. Looking past the labels that write people off as unable to contribute forms an important part of the shift in perspective from "We are a broken community filled with needs" to "We are a community filled with gifts".

My daughter Annie is a person with a wonderful sense of humor, infectious enthusiasm, good heart, kindness, and a beautiful smile. She is also a person with an intellectual disability who has been labeled "mentally retarded". Often people see her only as disabled rather than seeing the many other gifts Annie offers. My dream has always been that Annie will get the chance to live a life where she is needed for her gifts. It is true that we all have the great need to be needed.

I once asked my friend John McKnight, "What will allow Annie to have a safe and secure future?" John said the problem is that people in everyday life don't know that they need Annie. They don't realize that without Annie present and contributing, none of us can have a whole community. If Annie has no meaningful place, then none of us has a place we can count on.

Exercise

Labels that Say a Person Has No Gifts.

In a small group, name as many labels as you can that say "he or she is not gifted." Some labels, like "mentally retarded" or "juvenile delinquent," come from helping professions. Some, like "gang banger" or " lazy bum," come from everyday community life.

Reflection: Use this space to record what you have learned from naming labels that exclude people's gifts from community life. How would your practice change if you wanted to connect with the gifts of people excluded by prejudice?

Comment: No one is just a label. People are always more than one thing. I may be a drunk and also a musician or a talented painter. Communities working to get stronger will not buy the deficiency view that any person is only a negative label with nothing to offer. Community builders are determined to find what else a person is, what he or she has to contribute.

Associations and Congregations

An association is a group of local citizens joined together with a vision of a common goal. Association members decide what they want to do, decide how they want to do it, and take action to *do it!* What distinguishes an association is that groups of people who are *not* paid to act together join into common purpose, sometimes with a small paid staff. Some associations are formal, like the Rotary Club, and many are informal, like my wife Carol's supper club. Associations are flexible and creative. Associations are great places for people to participate and to contribute. Associations are amplifiers of individual gifts, in which individuals who want to participate are usually welcomed and encouraged to contribute. Associations can reach out into the community to engage large numbers of people in ways that will positively affect their attitudes and behaviors.

Religious congregations are a particularly valuable kind of local association. Congregations are very important because they are based on good values and have some permanence. A congregation can also be thought of as an "association of associations," comprising the choir, youth group, prayer group, men's and women's groups, and others.

Associations are already organized groups of individuals. These groups are an asset to community work because they are made up of connected people who are already doing something meaningful to them. They have the possibility to expand or change focus and do something different in the future. It is often

Powers of Associations (Often unrecognized)
- **Effective in action**
- **Amplifier of gifts**
- **Creative**
- **Reach large numbers**

Types of Voluntary Community Associations

Artistic Organizations: Rock bands, dance groups, theater groups

Business Organizations: Chamber of Commerce, neighborhood business associations

Charitable Groups and Drives: Red Cross, AIDS Task Force, Cancer Society, Salvation Army

Church Groups: Altar Society, Bible study groups, choir

Community Support Groups: Friends of the Library, Historic Preservation Society

Seniors Groups: Grey Panthers, America Association of Retired Persons

Interest Groups: Car and motorcycle clubs, recycling groups, writer's groups and book clubs

Informal Support Networks: Kinship networks, informal groups of neighbors, relatives and friends

Mutual Support: adoptive and foster parent groups, AA,, La Leche, Habitat for Humanity

Neighborhood Groups: Block watch, neighborhood associations

Outdoor Groups: Garden clubs, Audubon Groups, Nature Conservancy

Political Organizations: Democrats, Republicans

Professional Organizations: Unions, Bar Association, Medical Society

School Groups: PTA, adopt a school groups, volunteer tutors

Service Clubs: Sertoma, Lions, League of Women Voters

Social Cause Groups: Stonewall Union, housing and hunger task forces, MAD., ARC.

Sports/Health Clubs: Sports leagues, runner's clubs

Youth Organizations: Scouts, 4-H, computer clubs

Source: J. Kretzmann & J. McKnight. (1993) *Building Community From the Inside Out.*

more efficient to engage groups of people who already know how to work together and then to invite others to join than to start with disconnected individuals. For example, in working for child literacy, it would be efficient to recruit five association groups, each with twenty members who can see the connection between literacy and their group's interests. This would engage a hundred people who already have relationships with other active citizens.

I once met a lady who described the evolution of her club, the Jacksonville Sailing Club. It used to be primarily a men's club, but over time, professional women became the majority of members. Now the club is still about sailing, but the members have a huge interest in connecting young women to local professions through mentoring and networking. So their brochure still says "Jacksonville Sailing Club", but a deeper purpose is helping young women succeed. You could only learn this deeper story in conversation with one of the leaders of the association. However frivolous or profound an association's stated purpose, there is always the future possibility that it can do something else or something more. Every association has both a present purpose and a future vision of what it might do, even if the future vision remains unspoken in the group until someone initiates a conversation about possibilities.

Working Gifts and Waiting Gifts

A woman in a congregation I was working with said to me, "You know, all of us have working gifts. These are gifts that we develop and strengthen throughout our lives. But we also have waiting gifts, gifts waiting to be called and developed. We don't often know what our waiting gifts are until we're pressed into service." I had never thought of it that way and I wonder how many of us think about what are our working gifts, and what are our waiting gifts.

–Henry Moore

Exercise:

How Many Associations Are You Connected To?

In a small group, list association connections for each person. 1) Identify all the associations that you or your loved ones are connected to. 2) Total the number of associations for all the people in your group. 3) Guess at the total number of individual members among all the associations on your group's list of associations.

Reflection: Use this space to record your thoughts about how you can use this idea of associations as a way to mobilize action.

Comment: A group of ten people might easily be connected to fifty associations with an average membership of twenty people in each, for a total of 1000 possible connections! People doing this exercise are often amazed by the number of people they are already linked to.

We are each more linked than we know, through a **Web of Connections**. This is the practical meaning of the idea that community development is relationship driven. Power in communities is power through relationships. This is where the energy to realize goals can always be found.

Any group can widen the exercise to total not just associations, but also all the connections that all members have to local groups of associations, congregations, businesses, and agencies. Once made visible, this web of connections can be used in many ways to organize powerful action together.

Exercise

Using a Web of Connections

Name as many ways as you can that a mapping out your "web of connections" could help your community-building group to engage your community. How might you use the relationships of trust, influence, and connection that the members of your group have?

Institutions

Institutions include businesses, nonprofit agencies, and government agencies. An institution organizes a group of people to produce something. Institutions focus on efficiently fulfilling their mission: paid workers deliver goods and services to paying customers or eligible clients. Institutions are organized for consistency, efficiency, and reliability. And, institutions can offer far more to communities getting stronger than is obvious until community leaders move beyond stated purposes and look at institutions as a treasure chest of assets. For example, schools are primarily for educating children. And schools also have many other assets to contribute to communities getting stronger: students, staff, parents, knowledge and expertise, networks of connections, materials and equipment, economic power, space, and facilities. When people start to look for assets, possibilities grow for partnerships that will strengthen both the community and its institutions. A school that opens its treasure chest to citizens working to build a better neighborhood will improve itself as well.

Institutions

Organized for Efficiency, Consistency, Reliability

Businesses • Schools • Parks * Libraries • Hospitals •
Non-profit Agencies • Governments

Exercise

A School as a Treasure Chest?

In a small group, brainstorm for twenty minutes about how many possible ways a school might contribute to its community getting stronger in addition to its mission to educate children.

Reflection: Use this space to write down some of your thoughts on how the idea of institutions as treasure chests could influence the ways you work to make your community stronger.

Local Economy

The local economy is how money flows through a community. Every social problem has an economic dimension. When a community is more connected socially, economic well being grows. What is good for a local community and good for a local economy are closely related. For example a "buy locally" campaign greatly strengthens a community: as locally owned businesses grow, local jobs develop, and people who work in the community contribute to the community as residents, members, and friends.

Physical World

The physical world, both the natural world, like fields and rivers, and the manufactured world, like roads and buildings, shapes the place in which a community grows. I have often observed that communities making progress often see new and unexpected uses for buildings and land. What seemed a "glass half empty" becomes a "glass half full". For example, the unused trash dump becomes a lively space for recycling.

Using What You Have to Create What You Want

Asset Based Community Development is an invitation to look at communities differently, to see then as places in which citizens can build a good future together by discovering local treasures, connecting people and associations, and providing opportunities for people to give their gifts. Communities become motivated by what they don't have to use what they do have in order to create what they want —by working together. That is the essence of ABCD.

Every community that is getting stronger has at its center an effort to build up a wider circle of people who choose to take action for the common good.

Stone Soup

The version of this old story that I want to offer is from Africa. I think its moral is, "It's amazing what you can do when people contribute their gifts and their talents together."

There was a traveler who had been traveling all day for several days and he came upon a lively market. He was very hungry and he walked up to one of the villagers and he said, "Sir, I'm so hungry I don't know what to do. Could you feed me tonight?" And the villager said to him, "I'm sorry, sir, but I hardly have enough to feed my own family. I can't help you." And he approached another villager and he got basically the same answer, "I'm sorry, sir, I can't help you. I hardly have enough to feed my family."

He was wondering what to do when he saw a rock shaped like a mango that gave him an idea, so he reached over and picked up the rock, and he climbed up on a crate, and he spoke to the people in the market. "Ladies and Gentlemen, with this stone I'm going to make some magic soup." And everybody started walking around him to see what he was going to do. And he said, "Now, I need a pot with some water." And so one lady said, "Well, my house is just across the road. We can walk over there and you can use mine." The group followed him across the road, they got the water boiling, and he ceremoniously placed the mango shaped stone into the pot of boiling water.

Then he said, "Now, stone soup is good all by itself, but if you really want to make it right, you need to add some carrots." And one lady said, "Well, I have some carrots." So they chopped up the carrots and put the carrots in. And then he said, "Now, stone soup with carrots is outstanding, but if you really want to make it better, you add some onions." And another guy walked forward and said, "I've got some onions and let's put them in." And so, one by one, the villagers began to add different ingredients to this soup. Pretty soon, everybody marveled at how a stranger had walked into the village and made enough soup so that everybody in the village had plenty to eat that evening.

When I think about that stone, it shows a way to use imagination to give people the chance to contribute what they have in a way that nourishes and strengthens everyone. When I think of this story, I think of how we in the ABCD world call gifts to the center of a community's awareness and efforts, and how doing this can bring people from isolation and scarcity to connection and sharing.

–Henry Moore

Beyond Welfare: Money, Meaning and Friends

Story County, Iowa has a population of just over 74,000, with the majority of those folks living in Ames, the county seat and home of Iowa State University. Less than 2% of those residents are people of color. There are 8,336 households in the county with incomes under $25,000. Nothing about those statistics stands out at first glance; Central Iowa is a mostly white place, and rural poverty is often hidden behind that homogeneity. But Story County is also home to a gathering of citizens who call themselves Beyond Welfare, an organization that brings down the walls between the hidden poor and the rest of the community.

Beyond Welfare states its goal simply: eliminate poverty in Story County by 2020. Ambitious? Maybe. But the manner in which Beyond Welfare is moving toward that goal makes its attainment seem possible. To eliminate poverty, Beyond Welfare is reweaving community; promoting a connected life filled with enough money, meaning and friends for all.

The Beyond Welfare folks call that their mantra –"we all need money, meaning and friends". But the inclusive implication of that mantra is startling. Poverty of life and experience can beset those who have enough money, but little meaning and few friends. So, there is something for everyone in the community built by Beyond Welfare.

"Everything We Do Is Intentional"

The founders of Beyond Welfare (BW) have thought long and hard about everything they do. There is a language and process that determines all of their actions. For example, the **service-based language of "client" and "provider" has been replaced by the much more inclusive language of "participant" and "ally".** Becoming part of Beyond Welfare requires the same intake interview for everyone, regardless of role or income.

In brief, here's how Beyond Welfare works. To become a participant, the individual head of household meets with a counselor for an intake interview. This process welcomes participants into community, assists them in identifying their strengths as well as challenges, and introduces them to the values of relationship, reciprocity and leadership development that infuse everything that BW does.

From: Susan A. Rans (2005). *Hidden Treasures: Building Community Connections by Engaging the Gifts of People on Welfare, People with Disabilities, People with Mental Illness, Older Adults, Young People.* Evanston, IL: ABCD Institute. ©2005, ABCD Institute, reproduced here by permission.

Family partners are also recruited, trained and supported for intentional friendships with BW participants that are based on common interests. The safety and stability, self-sufficiency, and well being of the BW participant family remain at the center, however. BW assists families that are particularly isolated in enlisting a Circle of Support, a group of 3-4 volunteers that meets monthly to understand and support the goals of the family.

Where there is often a deficit of natural supports in families' lives, Family Partners and Circles of Support members help provide these supports in Family Team Meetings, designed to plan and work towards child and family safety.

On Thursday nights, BW hosts the Community Leadership Team, with a community meal followed by a meeting that focuses alternately on interdependent self-sufficiency and advocacy issues. On Thursdays, participants, family partners and allies all work together to support individual members' goals as well as group advocacy efforts. The value of the Thursday night meeting cannot be overstated; the coming-together of the entire community to share a meal and the joys and pains of the week has a ceremonial, if not liturgical feel to it. "Everything we do is intentional," says Lois Smidt, BW's co-founder and guiding light. "It all serves to build reciprocal, supportive relationships."

Removing Obstacles

BW understands that families in poverty have obstacles that range from employment difficulties to transportation. Available to participants is a range of opportunities to remove these obstacles.

- BW has an Employment Specialist who works with individual families on GED, job readiness, placement, and retention, as well as with employers, to help pave the way for hiring of our participants.

- Our Employment Specialist also voluntarily supports a computer lab, in partnership with local faith organizations. This lab is entirely staffed by volunteers, community members at large as well as BW participants.

- Wheels to Work, a car donation program, engages the broader community in a concrete, meaningful way (they can donate their cars), as well as meeting a concrete need identified by participant families.

- BW staff includes a Family Financial Planning Specialist who assists in financial literacy and planning, as well as Earned Income Tax Credit (EITC). She also trains and supports family partners in budget and EITC, so that they can support their BW partnering families in maximizing their opportunities and potential.

Community Context

As with everything else they do, the BW folks are careful never to stray too far from the citizen-centered heart of the endeavor. The very small BW staff is committed to

> …*community engagement to build the capacity of ordinary unpaid community members to be involved in making Story County a safer, friendlier, and more supportive community for all its members. By engaging people and the community at large in this way, we strive to build a countywide community where all of us have enough money, healthy relationships, and a sense of purpose and meaning."*
>
> *At the same time we are facilitating relationships that assist and support individual families, we are building a constituency of caring for the concerns of families at risk due to poverty and the harms associated with insufficient income, a constituency for changing attitudes, human service practice, and policies." (*<u>What Beyond Welfare Does</u>*, Lois Smidt and Scott Miller)*

Finally, BW is governed by a local community-lead Board of Directors, constituted by at least 51% members who have been or are currently marginalized by poverty.

Based in Experience

The remarkable framework of BW is the creation of the personal experience of Lois Smidt. Having spent several years on welfare in the 90's, Lois is keenly aware of the struggles and pitfalls of trying to raise a family in poverty. Isolation, suppressed anger, stereotypes—all seem to get in the way of even the most determined attempt to overcome them. "Although I certainly had many supportive relationships in my life by this time, as well as community involvement and support, I was still bombarded with patterns of worthlessness and helplessness that were reinforced by reliance on public assistance and the attitudes projected by human service providers and the general public," she says.

Two experiences while on welfare profoundly affected her ability to leave it: one, with a Family Development Specialist from Mid-Iowa Community Action (MICA) and the other as a member of an artist's collective of women.

The attitude of MICA and its workers was one of respect and one that stressed Lois' strengths. No experience she had previously had with the service industry came close to providing this. In addition, Cindy, the specialist, provided unwavering respect and support to Lois and her family. "It was the knowledge that there was another human being, particularly one who worked for an agency funded by government, who was deeply interested in my development and held forth her belief in my capacity most profoundly. This provided for me feelings of worth, value, safety, and competence that had yet to be paralleled," says Lois.

Lois Smidt

Similarly, when she attended a workshop for No Limits for Women in the Arts, Lois found a creative and supportive environment that crossed race and class lines. She soon began a local support group for women artists as a part of No Limits. "I built relationships with women across class and race lines that fundamentally contradicted the feelings of worthlessness, helplessness, and discouragement that are reinforced by living on welfare," she says. "I was supported and propelled into leadership. This required that I give up internalized patterns of insignificance that fuel social stereotypes about welfare moms. For two years I met with women twice a month to ask each other questions such as – 'What is your biggest vision for your art and your life? What is your next step? What is in your way? What support do you need to make sure you don't stop?' These questions were asked in the context of intentional listening and unconditional belief in our intelligence to figure things out."

These two ideas –that relationships are essential and that respectful, supportive connections can cross barriers and build leadership– became cornerstones of Lois' work and that of BW. She later encountered the concepts of Reconstructive Co-Counseling (RC) that provided her with tools and exercises that support her vision. The tools and principles of co-counseling aim to break down the barriers caused by race and class by engaging in the tough work of one-to-one listening and support. They can be found in use most especially on Thursday Nights, at the Community Team Meeting.

The Train and the Brakes

Scott Miller came to MICA by a circuitous route. His privileged background had done little to prepare him for a bout of depression in his first year of college, and that experience led him to think about the relationship between mental health and connected life. He was drawn to community organizing, and found he had a special skill at initiating projects and finding creative ways to fund them.

MICA's Family Development concept, a program that went into homes with families, and assisted them to write action contracts to get out of poverty, was radical for the social service world; Scott came to work there because of it. This was how he met Lois, who had gone to work as a Family Development Specialist with the hope of extending the same strength-based support she had received.

Scott noticed her work with welfare women and her energy, and she noticed that he knew lots about raising money. But she also noticed he seemed a bit disillusioned, and she knew about co-counseling. So, they had a significant amount of possible reciprocal exchange, she thought, and she initiated conversation with him. "I went to him and said, hey you know something that I want to know and I think I can teach you a few things, too. And it just went from there."

Scott saw that the welfare world was changing, and he felt a new approach was needed. "TANF was coming down the pike—this was 1996. So we said why don't we try something that builds relationships to try to eliminate poverty?" says Scott. And ultimately, Beyond Welfare was born.

Scott and Lois are still at the center of BW. "Scott and I laugh about that. We say he's the train and I'm the brakes," says Lois. And the barriers and difficulties they have encountered in their relationship have served as a template for BW. "We are the perfect model of difficulties encountered building relationships across class lines. We are very conscious of it. We think if we are having this problem, then maybe allies and participants might have it too."

Allies

As BW developed, it attracted a core group of people for whom the idea of building relationships to eliminate poverty made sense. One of them, Terry Pickett, speaks eloquently about his role as a Family Partner. "I now lead a much richer social life. I have a more interesting and challenging social group and I am engaged in my community in much richer ways than the average middle class white male."

Terry, once a communications professor at ISU, is now a business consultant. About three years ago he made a commitment to semi-retire in order to spend about half his time "in the community". "I wanted to do corporal work, not be a facilitator, which is what I do for a living. I wanted to give back to those who were on the margins." He has been deeply involved in BW for three years, including as a member of its board.

Terry has written a piece for BW called "The Evolution of Helping", in which he tries to unpack what it is he can bring. "I won't deny my competency—I do know things that they would benefit from knowing: how to do long-range planning, how to arrange my finances." But it is about the relationship, according to Terry. And not just for the participant. "I have needs I am bringing to the relationship, too. Not around money, but around friendship. On a personal level, the relationships I have in this community (as opposed to my neighborhood, where everyone is like me) are much more vulnerable

For Terry Pickett's reflections on BW, turn to page xxx.

which makes them much more relaxing. I don't have to be competent at everything. And that's affected my other relationships as well."

Steve Ainger is the current board chair, and the BW researcher. As a Political Scientist at ISU, he has the tools to produce data about BW that is necessary for foundations and other outside agencies. Personally, Steve says, "These are all my friends now. I could move, take another job, but how could I take Beyond Welfare with me?" He says that lots of theoretical literature talks about transformative, reciprocal relationship building as essential to community, but "Beyond Welfare walks the talk."

As Pastor of Collegiate Presbyterian Church, Vickie serves as host to the Thursday night BW gatherings. She describes her calling to social justice as beginning in her rural childhood, and carrying into her church during the sixties when she was in high school. When she grew up and discovered that not all churches had stressed the same kind of commitment to justice, she set out to try to change that.

That effort led to frustration, mostly, until she began to work with BW "because they deal with the whole person and they focus on the importance of relationships." She stressed the importance of the systems approach to poverty: "It's not just about money; it understands the importance of support."

She is a Family Partner to an undocumented Guatemalan woman who has "all the issues around being undocumented in this climate". She admires her participant's resourcefulness even while she gets frustrated with recurring problems. "I like BW because we are in it for the long haul. I like being around people who think they can eliminate poverty. And the great thing is that whatever skill is brought forward, there's always someone who needs it—participants or partners. We all gain from each other's knowledge. I really like the reciprocity."

Participants

Liz is a single mom with a teenage son. She lives on the outskirts of Ames with her mother who has Altzheimer's and requires constant care. Liz cares for her mom even though she has little money, because she is a Korean adoptee, and she credits her mom with sacrificing for her and saving her life. To pay for the care and medication needed by her mom, Liz works two restaurant jobs, often double shifts. "Some months the cost of her care is more than I make; some months we do OK," she says. "But I'd never make it if it weren't for the car."

Liz has a 1992 Nissan Sentra hatchback wagon, big enough to fold her mom's wheelchair into. The car was donated to her through BW's "Wheels to Work" program. "Without a car I had to take her on the bus to adult day care, then take the bus back to my job. That took two hours." Wheels to Work cars are not free; participants have to pay for insurance and upkeep, and they have to agree not to let anyone else borrow the car until they have had it for 18 months. They also have to reciprocate, a key element in BW's philosophy. "I only pay $5 a month for the car, but I sign a paper saying I'll contribute so many hours in return." So Liz volunteers at a church child care center, tending to kids while their moms learn English. " I love kids," she says. "I look forward to that time so much." The moms are Korean, Chinese, Latino and Turkish. "Because I'm Korean, it's easy for them to trust me."

Liz provides support to many in return for the support she is given. She finds time to take two neighbors without cars to the store to shop for groceries. "We fill up the back of that car with food. I think they picked that car just for me, so I could fit all that stuff in."

Transportation is important to folks. Liz thinks. "I do know people without a home, but cars are a biggie. I know a mom who pulled her kids out of Head Start—she couldn't keep spending two hours a day on the bus, getting up at 5 AM to get the right bus, just to get her kids to school."

Liz's Circle of Support assists her with her many responsibilities. One member helps with her financial planning, helping her keep a budget and make out her checks for her bills every month. "She tells me not to give my money away—I'm always giving it away to friends and family who need it. She also keeps me from the pay loan store in the bad months."

"My mom's medication costs $600 a month, so most of what I make goes to care for her. Some people ask me, 'Don't you get depressed? Don't you get down?' But I don't. I just keep going. My faith helps me, and my Circle is there."

A Thursday Night Meeting

Preceding the actual meeting is a communal supper. Prepared and served by BW participants and allies, the meal serves as a kind of ritual that calls the community together. Of course, it is very hard to tell who's who and that's the point. Lots of little kids are carefully watched by a bunch of teens; greetings and hugs all around; that church-basement-fellowship feeling abounds. Everyone greeted Lois upon entry —there was a sense that the proceedings could now begin.

Upstairs, the meeting took place in a large room, with chairs in a circle. Probably 30 or so folks participated, the kids stayed in another room with folks to care for them and keep an eye on them. Having time away from the kids was clearly relaxing for their parents, and that made the meeting a comfortable space.

Lois opened the meeting, reminding everyone of the rules of the meeting: confidentiality, safe space, support, listening. Then the room was circled twice: once for celebrations and once for concerns. Listening to the positives and the troubles made it a bit clearer who was who in the room, but by that time it really didn't make a difference. And the powerful honesty displayed by all who spoke was striking. Little victories brought genuine joy, and thorny problems or worries were brainstormed, with volunteered assistance often being the result.

As part of the meeting, everyone did a 'listening pair', a period of focused, non-judgmental listening between two people. Then, information was exchanged in a bulletin board format and the meeting ended with Appreciations, a time when each person was asked to appreciate the person next to them.

Lois made it clear that some form of all of these things happen at each meeting. The ritualized nature of the whole thing is meant to be safe and comforting, so that trust can increase and become the norm. Thursday nights are central for most people, like a weekly gathering of friends that provides support, relief and safety.

During the meeting, one person was articulate and passionate, and seemed extremely connected to the entire BW vision. Her name was Nou Mous. She is Hmong, but her name is French. "It means 'No More'; I was the last of nine children." She is 21, and she has been involved with BW for two years. She came to Ames from California originally to help a friend living with mental illness. She soon found herself with a small child and no resources. "No one ever prepares for poverty, " she says. "No on ever thinks they could be homeless one day." She saw a pamphlet for BW at a laundromat; she was skeptical.

"It said they help with job counseling and emotional support and finances and that you could get a car, and I thought, 'it's a cult'." But, it was a cult with a car program, so she took her doubts and went to a meeting. And everything about Beyond Welfare made sense to her. "It's the support you get, the friends you make, being intentional about it. We've carved this place in our lives on Thursday nights for BW. The first night when I heard the rules, I thought 'this just makes sense'."

So she got a Circle of Support and got a car and decided it might not be a cult. "At my first session with my Circle of Support, I was shocked. No one had ever asked me 'what are your dreams?' And at the time, my dream was to pay my bills, keep gas in my car, keep my daughter, find a job. I didn't even realize I had stopped dreaming."

She had never finished high school in California; she was two classes shy. Within one month, she received her high school diploma. That was March of 2002. Today, she is a full-time student, working on a degree in technical writing and communications. She plans on graduate school, "possibly law school if I want to really get suicidal."

"I feel like it wasn't an accident that I am here, and I want to spread the message of BW everywhere, to the world. I want to take it to a Third World country, to take my gifts to Asia where my roots are. I feel like I am here for a reason."

"I'm a pretty big advocate," she adds.

"You know, somebody's story needs to be told. I wasn't really keen on being a poster child for poverty, but it just worked out that way. I just happen to have a gift for public speaking, for expressing a story."

She sees it as a commitment to her daughter, a daughter she almost gave up for adoption. "Now, I'm doing this for her. To make this a better place for her." She credits her Circle of Support with helping her leave the mentality of poverty. And she describes the circle as "a big bulls-eye with you in the middle", constantly changing roles but always there. "Just like life." It was making a connection with people, as she never had a nuclear family's support, and "it was having safe people to come around my daughter."

Nou Mous is fiercely protective of her daughter, having felt what lack of protection can be like. "It's important to me. She doesn't have to be the adult in this relationship." Lois and Matt, another BW ally, are her daughter's godparents. "Single parents don't have the luxury of not planning in case something goes wrong. I know she will be brought up well if something happens."

"But that is what Beyond Welfare has done for me, helped me be someone who has plans for her life, for her daughter, for school. It isn't perfect; sometimes we have to call each other out when stuff is going on. But I am comfortable with that; I am comfortable with expressing my feelings now."

Her daughter came into the room, and they embraced and laughed. Nou Mou is a young woman who found her voice, her support, and a meaning for her life. Money, meaning and friends.

Lessons Learned from Beyond Welfare

- The initiators had both experienced marginalization—Lois as a welfare recipient and Scott as someone who had experienced mental illness. They used these experiences as a touchstone in every part of Beyond Welfare.

- Everything done by Beyond Welfare is intentional, voluntary and volitional. A participant can choose how much to get involved, but complete involvement is a tremendous commitment. The payoff is tremendous transformation for all.

- Beyond Welfare is, at its core, citizen-centered. It is very careful to maintain this commitment in all things.

- Beyond Welfare comfortably and self-consciously uses and improvises from other programs and practices, especially co-counseling, but also 12-step programs.

- Beyond Welfare is very specific about its goal (ending poverty) and its objectives (money, meaning, friends).

- Beyond Welfare is also very specific, almost liturgical, about its practices: dream paths, the Thursday meetings, Circles of Support, Family partners, listening pairs, questioning the "boundary" (between social service and community).

- Membership in Beyond Welfare is explicit; there is a sense of belonging to something.

- All of this specificity makes the Beyond Welfare program transportable to other communities and teachable.

An important footnote: Interest in Beyond Welfare has brought about the institution of a Beyond Welfare Training component, and that component is being led by Lois Smidt. She is traveling to other states now, and is in less day-to-day contact. Lois is no longer the Connector—she creates the context for connecting, as the organizer and teacher, but the work of connecting is shared by other Beyond Welfare members.

In addition, Beyond Welfare is expanding to Des Moines, a much larger community than Ames and the state capitol. Significant funding support and institutional buy-in from the Des Moines school system has encouraged this expansion. Scott Miller is excited about the possible opportunities involved in this new project, but knows they will be challenged by it.

Beyond Welfare
130 S. Sheldon Ave. Suite #302
Ames, IA 50014
(515)292-5992

www.beyondwelfare.org

If It's Rats, It's Rats!

   I went to Norfolk, Virginia, several years ago to work with a
fellow by the name of Curtis Randolph, who was director of
Neighborhood Services. I was training department heads, helping them to transform the city organization, to lead by stepping back, and to think about how to lift citizens up and support
them in their work.

   One of the interesting things Curtis told me was that the mayor had won a recent
election, and part of his platform was to clean up the public housing project, a project that had a reputation for drugs and crime and so forth. So they had been out
meeting with citizens and talking with them about cleaning up the neighborhood.
But there was a problem: citizens would come to meetings but they didn't seem to
make a lot of progress on the city official's agenda for cleaning up drugs and crime.

   After a number of conversations, they discovered that people in the neighborhood
saw a problem with rats. There were a lot of young mothers with babies, and people
were fearful that the rats might get in the crib or get in the bed. In fact, they told
of an occasion when a rat was seen in the crib, although that time the baby wasn't
harmed. This information led city staff to help public housing residents work to bait
the rats. Over a period of six or nine months, they cleaned up the rat problem. And
then they noticed that, after the rats problem had been abated, citizens in the public
housing complex began to get more involved in a number of neighborhood improvement
initiatives, including cleaning up drugs and crime.

   To me, the moral of this story is, if people tell you the problem is rats, then the problem is rats. It's not crime or drugs, even if crime and drugs seems like the problem to
you. Sometimes it's hard for those of us in authority to believe that it's rats because
our briefcases are so full with statistics about crime and drugs and answers to the
crime and drugs problem that we can't hear that citizens want to begin with rats.
If we want to succeed at mobilizing citizens, we have to close up our briefcase full of
answers for a while and open up our ears.

                                                                    –Henry Moore

III

The Song of Community
What People Care About Enough To Act

There is no power for change greater than a community discovering what it cares about.

-Margaret Wheatley

People in *every* community care about something

The most important asset in any community is people's willingness to act on what they care about. Care brings people together for common purpose. Care is a song that flows through every community and those who want to develop stronger communities must know how to recognize it and harmonize with it. The song of community becomes more audible to leaders willing to ask simple questions and listen thoughtfully to the answers:

• What *do* you care about?

• What will you *do* about that?

Community: A Place Filled With Care

- Care remains invisible without intentional conversations about what people care about.

- People may not care about what those with a particular agenda want them to care about.

- Care must be discovered through relationships that are built on purpose.

- Learning conversations are the way to make care visible

When the song of care is clearly heard, people find the power to act together. Those who want to help often try to get community members to do things that helper's think they should do, based on the helper's problem analysis. If, as often happens, the helpers find no response they conclude that citizens don't care. They apply labels like "unmotivated," "in denial," and "at risk" to a place because *they* can't hear the song of community there. But the reality is different. People not caring about what others want them to care about is a different kind of problem from people not caring. Some conclude that no one cares, but **in twenty-five years of community work I have never seen a community where people don't care about something!** When communities are not responsive to a particular agenda, this does not mean that people do not care. It is more a problem of poor listening to the community than a problem of low motivation in the community.

Learning Conversations

Care and motivation are revealed through intentional learning conversations rather than through data collection. Impersonal studies can show what assets are in a community but not what people will do with what they have.

Agencies often miss this simple fact. Helpers want to survey a community to find out what is important to people. But the problem with surveys is that they do not reveal people's motivation —whether people are really ready to act and under what circumstances they will act.

Motivation to Act vs Opinion

Discovering what a person is motivated to act on requires deep listening and careful watching to find out what each particular person cares about, how they care, and how much. It's easy to misjudge motivation to act. A community meeting of 50 people can set a priority to do something important, such as tutoring young people, but a week later only four people show up when the tutoring group meets. This is not a fault of the people at the big meeting, it is a failure to accurately **distinguish between opinion and motivation to act.** Opinion is what I want *someone* to do. Motivation to act is what I will *do* myself. Learning conversations are the only effective way to distinguish opinion from motivation to act.

Three forces fuel motivation to act. First, people act on **concerns**: what they don't want to happen. Second, people act on **dreams and goals**: what they want to create. Third, people may act when there is an **opportunity to contribute their gifts** in a particular way. Think about the issue of young people succeeding. Many people will act on concerns about violence, school dropout rates, or drugs. Many people will work for the shared goals of better economic opportunities and for improved high school graduation rates. Some people may get involved in particular activities that provide an opportunity to give one of their gifts, for example a person may volunteer to tutor because she wants an opportunity to teach.

Learning Conversations

Care = Motivation to Act: "What I will go out the door and do something about"

- Concerns – What I don't want to happen

- Dreams –What I want to create

- Gifts – What I want the opportunity to give

Distinguish Motivation to Act ("I will …") from Opinion ("Somebody ought to…")

Exercise

Learning Conversations To Discover Motivation To Act

Two people have a 30-minute conversation in which each listens to the other for 10 minutes and both take the final 10 minutes for discussion.

First, based on listening to what the other person says about what is really important, each identifies one strong motivation to act for the other person: What does the other person really care about enough to take action?

Second, reflect together on the discussion and see if you can notice how you identify something the other person really cares about and not just an opinion. How do you know when you hear the difference between opinion and motivation to act?

Discussion questions

- What was it like to ask another person about what was really important to her or him?
- What was it like to be asked about what was really important to you?
- How did you recognize real "motivation to act" rather than just an "opinion"?
- How could you see using these kinds of learning conversations to discover what people care about- enough to act?

Reflection: Use this space to record your most important insight into discovering care in your community.

Comment: People typically find this kind of 1:1 conversation fun, energizing, even inspiring. People rarely consider this kind of conversation an imposition. When you ask another person what is most important to him or her, you are taking another person very seriously as a valuable human being. People often find that this kind of conversation clarifies priorities. People in these conversations usually find common ground and feel more connected to each other.

Start with the Question

To find motivation to act start with a question about what the other person cares about, not your own answer. Don't impose your solutions. Mobilize other's motivation to act. This attitude opens a space for the other person to say, "Yes, I want to do something about this issue and here is what I want to do." For example, a helper could decide that tutoring is the answer to the problem of literacy and try to recruit a lot of people to be tutors. Some will say "yes" and some will say "no". The helper could easily conclude that those who say "no" do not care about literacy. But many people may just not care to tutor. They may be willing to take some other action if the space is opened for them: making translations, forming reading groups, helping at libraries, and a hundred other possibilities. So coming to people with a question –"What do you want to do to increase literacy?"– will discover much more care and mobilize more action than bringing an answer: tutoring. Helpers who try to control community members to implement and consume professional answers miss the opportunities to strengthen community that come up when community members are engaged as citizens who act together to address a question that matters to them.

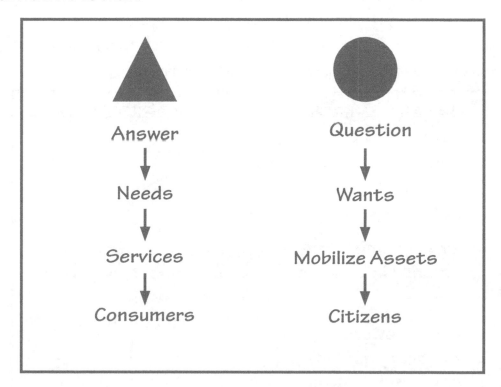

When I was trained as a social worker, I was taught to assess what a client needed, decide on an intervention to meet that need and then deliver the matching service. Many times people did not respond to what I did, and I often diagnosed them as unmotivated or resistant. Later, I became a community organizer and learned to work in the opposite way: always starting with a question to discover what people wanted. In my first year of organizing I often went to my boss and said, "I want to work on this issue." He always said the same thing, "Who told you to do it? How many people in the neighborhood will work on this issue?" If I could not clearly identify a lot of local people who were motivated to act on an issue, I could not organize on the issue –no matter how important it seemed to me. Later I came to realize how strange it is that professionals in the helping world so often do things that they think people need without having any idea whether the people affected care enough about the answer to act to get it.

> **To mobilize a community, never do anything nobody wants!**

Letting go of having the answer and refraining from blaming people for not accepting your answer can be painful. Starting from where people are and not where you wish they were requires receptivity and creativity. But the gain is worth the pain. The answers about how to engage a community are found in learning conversations with people from that community.

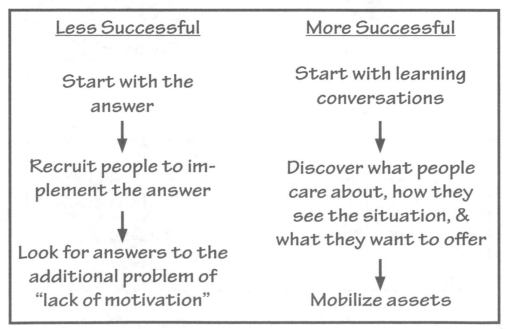

<u>Less Successful</u>	<u>More Successful</u>
Start with the answer	Start with learning conversations
↓	↓
Recruit people to implement the answer	Discover what people care about, how they see the situation, & what they want to offer
↓	↓
Look for answers to the additional problem of "lack of motivation"	Mobilize assets

From Individual Interests to Common Interest.

As individual motivation to act is identified through listening to several people, a pattern often emerges that weaves individual interests into common interest. Shifting from outside-in diagnoses of problems and prescriptions of answers to inside-out questions about care makes it clear who is ready to act together, and for which set of diverse reasons. For example there are many different individual reasons parents, teachers, students, and neighbors might join together to build a stronger local school.

People are more alike than different at the level of what is really important, such as ensuring children's safety. When a group of people have done one-to-one learning conversations to discover a variety of individual interests they generally find a clear path to common interest by reflecting together on what they have heard. This process of finding common interest does not require statistical analysis but simply thoughtful discussion among people who have had learning conversations with their fellow citizens.

Exercise

Common Interest from Individual Interests.

Work in a group of three people for ten minutes. Find three interests that all of you share and that each of you already act on. These interests can be in any area of your life outside the requirements of your job.

Reflection: Use this space to record your most important learning about weaving individual interests into common interests.

Connector Leaders

Connector leaders are the key to mobilizing people to act together on what they care about. Connector leaders have earned trust, influence, and a following among citizens. They have the relationships necessary to bring citizens together in ways that create the opportunities to act on care that make a community's assets productive. The right five to ten people can build a community partnership that works if they will call on the trust they have built among the people in their relationship circles.

I used to be a salesman. What sales people hate more than anything are cold calls. You don't want to go anywhere that nobody sent you. You always want to be sent by someone who is connected to a place, has the ability to open the door, and can lend you her or his trust and influence.

Don't go anywhere that nobody sent you.

The same thing is true in developing community. I once worked with a wonderful connector leader in Commerce City, near Denver. Beth would give me a list of people to contact. As soon as I told them that Beth sent me, people immediately were warm and receptive to whatever I asked. One person said to me, "Everyone in town owes Beth. She has helped so many people over so many years. If Beth asks you to do something, you do it." One way you know you have met a connector leader is that people in their community keep saying, "Have you talked to Beth? You need to meet Beth. Beth will know what to do and who to see." There are people like Beth in every community. These people are not necessarily office holders or recognized, out-in-front leaders. Connector leaders may be very quiet and soft-spoken and work in the background, but each one has a strong circle of relationships that they can and will call upon when something truly matters to them.

When I talked about connector leaders in a workshop in New Hampshire, a person in the group said, "This reminds me of how you call ducks. To get the right ducks, you need the right duck call." The right ducks are well-connected people. The right duck call is discovering what they care about enough to act.

Exercise

Connector Leaders You Know

In a group of three, describe some connector leaders you know personally. People who are trusted, influential, and have a following in your community. Tell each other about your experiences with one of these connector leaders.

- Whom do you know who is a connector leader?
- How do you know when you have found a connector leader?
- What do you do to involve connector leaders?

Reflection: Use this space to record what you have learned by thinking about connector leaders. What personal qualities do you need to draw on and develop in order to earn their trust and gain influence with them?

To Get The Right Ducks, You Need the Right Duck Call

A community is mobilized through relationships and motivation to act

The right ducks – Connector leaders who have trust, influence, and a following.

The right duck call – Discovering what connector leaders care about enough to act,

Listening – Inside and Out

Mike Mather

Broadway (www.broadwayumc.org/) is a wonderfully diverse congregation in terms of ethnicity, culture, economics, age, political persuasion, sexuality, gender identity and theology. It is an eclectic mix of folk. We are a metropolitan congregation situated in a low-income inner city neighborhood.

Like many other main stream Protestant churches we have faced issues of a reduction of numbers of people in our congregation. At the same time, the people who are here are an incredibly vibrant, rich group. Sometimes folks who have been around here for a long time wish for the good old days. But mostly we revel in our life together.

We have made a deep commitment to listening to each other –to listening for what each other care about and what the gifts are that we bring to our shared life together. In the body of the congregation this has meant a pretty radical restructuring of our life together. If we were going to listen to one another, and build off of one another's shared gifts and concerns, how would we do that? First, we did it by changing the "old nominating committee" into a committee that saw that its first responsibility was to have conversations with people in and around the life of our congregation.

We got rid of all of our "program" committees and simply said that if there were not three people called and committed to carrying out something in the life of the church, we simply wouldn't do it anymore. We created one new, very small committee called **The Animators of the Spirit**. This three person committee only meets when called upon. They meet with people who are feeling an urging to take action based on their gifts and what they care about. The Animators do three things:

- They ask discerning questions;

- They point out where dragons lie (where they see stumbling blocks)

- They pray for and encourage people in their ministry.

These things have begun to strengthen our sense that we shouldn't do something if there aren't people committed to do it ("Don't do something that nobody wants") and that what we will do is act, and act quickly, on what people feel called to do. This has created a very

> **Instead of being seen as the "charity" church, we are making a transition to being seen as "the investment church" –the church who will invest in your dreams.**

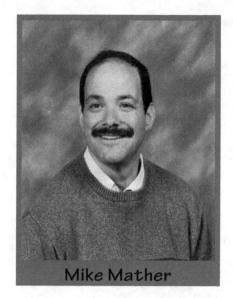

Mike Mather

real sense of energy and commitment on the part of people who see that they are being listened to and valued in ways that enrich our common life.

We also made a commitment to celebrate three things: the things that we had done in the past we were no longer doing, the ministries that are continuing, and ministries that are beginning.

We have also made a commitment to listening outside our walls as well as inside. In our local community we partnered with the local development corporation, which was in the midst of a strategic planning process, to hire someone we called **The Roving Listener.** The Roving Listener (De'Amon Harges) takes a block each week and talks with each person who lives on that block. He listens for the same things we listen for in the church. He listens for people's gifts —their interests, passions and where they are ready to act. The Roving Listener prepares a report every week on what he has heard, and he shares it with the development corporation for use in their strategic plan and with the congregation.

What has happened is that we have started having more and more people come to meet with the Animators of the Spirit to share both what they are doing and their dream about how to build on what they are already doing. Instead of being seen as the "charity" church, we are making a transition to being seen as "the investment church." That is to say that we are the church who will invest in your dreams – we are the place where you can come share what you believe is possible.

As a result of the restructuring and listening, we are discovering that the power in being heard is a wondrous thing. Rather than going to another meeting, people are actively engaged in the life of the neighborhood and the congregation and have found that it has improved the understanding of all who are engaged. We are part and parcel of an unfolding that portends to continue to foster the celebration of that which we enjoy in common.

These efforts to re-order our life together toward listening to one another and organizing to make sure that what comes out of these conversations is acted upon has re-vitalized our life together. It has lifted our spirits by reminding us of the goodness and richness of our lives and what we care about. And it reminds us that we are not alone.

Reflections From One Australian's ABCD Journey
Ted Smeaton

Because ABCD is about building on success and relationships, it is hard to know where such a journey starts and ends. What is mine or any one person's contribution to a community discovering its strengths, hopes and power is often hard to work out. Any community organizing effort, by its nature, has many partners, innovators and builders. A number of people from public housing estates who innately understood ABCD principles, as well as talented community connectors/organizers and leading practitioners, have shaped and will continue to shape my journey.

As a young community educator for people with disabilities I traveled for a week with John O'Brien through New South Wales (NSW), exploring the possibilities for people labeled with a disability who were returning home after living in large institutions. Spending time with these people, and being supported by John to reflect on what was possible, made me understand that every person has something to offer to their community and communities are much stronger when everyone is able to contribute.

This simple but profound lesson helped to guide the next 10 years of my life. During this period I worked at the Intellectual Disability Rights Service, helped establish the Disability Discrimination Legal Services, supported the first self-advocacy group in Australia for people labeled with intellectual disabilities, advocated for the rights of Indigenous Australians labeled with an intellectual disability and worked with Indigenous communities on social justice and community-owned and developed justice programs.

During this time I came across the concepts of ABCD and slowly took on the principles in my work. I also partnered with like-minded practitioners. ABCD practice wisdom has assisted in many community organizing efforts including these.

A simple conversation about skills, talents and passions, and a local single mum in a public housing estate on her back step saying "I can cook", led to the collective establishment of CCC catering, a small company owned and run by women who lived on the estate. Redefining rundown public houses as places of work and unemployed people as an under-utilized workforce created jobs for people in the housing estate.

Redefining local children as assets rather than trouble makers led to the development of an Independent Learning Centre - a computer centre where young people have access to internet, mentoring and learning opportunities. The Centre was designed by local kids and built by members of the senior citizens club. The local high school provided computer support, local businesses provided equipment and the Chamber of Commerce provided funding.

Ted Smeaton

The desire for community members to tell good rather then bad news stories about where they lived led to the development of The WAVE Community Newspaper. These are just a few examples of things that have grown from hope, real partnerships and noticing what works and the assets we can build upon.

On the Central Coast of NSW, where I now work, a number of people realized that telling government how bad the community was did not get them money or services and just made the community workers in the region feel demoralised.

They discovered the ABCD concept and formed the Central Coast Community Congress. The aim of the Congress is to develop the region from the inside out by talking about and building on what works. The Congress partnered with communities, agencies, government and local business to get connected, and, over the last five years, many things have happened. We have organized three congresses for local people to discover more about community building and celebrate 'real people doing real things'. Each congress has had more then 250 people attend and this has been a springboard for hope and change. .

The Benevolent Society, Australia's first and oldest community organization –and a key partner in the Congress– seeks to tackle social inequality by building caring and inclusive communities. The Society achieves this by delivering a range of programs and services, by working with communities to develop innovative solutions to complex social challenges, and by calling for a more just society.

A new part of The Benevolent Society's journey is the establishment of two 'Communities for Children' projects – one in western Sydney and one on the Central Coast. These projects, funded by the Australian Government, facilitate a community development approach to improving outcomes for children and families. We identify and support community connectors who will link new parents to each other and the community. We have a small grants program through which any two people can get funds to develop an idea that will make a child-friendly community where every child can reach their potential. The new group can then apply for a slightly bigger grant to help them turn their ideas and vision into reality. They are also encouraged to attend an organizing course to help them develop practical skills to design and implement their vision and weave a connected community. This concept is based on ideas shared with us by Mike Green.

A number of local community organizers and connectors hope that we will develop our own network to promote and support the role that community organizing can play in assisting communities to recognise and organise community assets to create caring and inclusive communities and a just society.

Our plan is that this network/centre would contribute to:

· Developing resources, mentoring education programs and supporting organizers to assist communities.

· Undertaking leading-edge research and disseminating the latest national and international research to practitioners, academics and governments.

· Facilitating and supporting the development of a National Network of Practice for community organizers.

· Advocating for new government support and increased funding.

· Engaging with the Corporate Sector to create partnerships for community organizing projects.

· Supporting exchange with practitioners from other countries ·

We trust that by building on our collective strengths and relationships and maintaining our hopeful optimism we will be able to turn this vision into reality.

PO Box 111 Wyong, NSW 2259

teds@bensoc.org.au

This Work Takes Time

Being a gapper isn't easy. Some people will accuse you of wasting time on building community. Others will think that you have some ulterior motive. Others will see a threat.

Sometimes I think about that old fable, the Scorpion and the Frog, because sometimes it seems that institutions –governments, schools, universities, businesses, agencies– are all about self-preservation. They're all about doing what they have to do. This is just the way it is.

They met on the bank of a stream and the scorpion asked the frog, "Could I get a ride across the stream on your back?" And the frog said, "Well, how do I know that you won't sting me?" And the scorpion said, "You know that if I do that, I'll die, too. We both will sink to the bottom of the river." And the frog says, "Well, yeah, that makes sense." And so they go across the river and they get about mid-way across the stream and Bam! the scorpion stings the frog. As the frog feels the onset of his paralysis and knows they're going to drown together, he says, "Just tell me one thing, why?" And the scorpion says, "Well, it's my nature."

The work inside of an organization takes time and there will be opponents. Some will be like the scorpion and think they just can't give up their top-down behaviors. Sometimes you've got to wait for people to retire, move to other jobs, or get forced out, before some parts of the organization will try leading by stepping back. But I believe that you have to work with whatever you have around you.

When my scope for action was limited, I just used whatever little control that I had to influence where I could, even when it was as few as one or two other people. This means it will take time for the work to grow, but once a few people on the inside feel valued and begin to see results they will develop a sense of ownership. Once you have a core of people trained, experienced and committed, then you can push the envelope. You have to continue to invest more in people, and it has to be known that it's okay to make mistakes as long as they just keep listening and keep supporting citizens.

–Henry Moore

Searching for the Right Relationship Between People and Programs

IV
People *and* Programs
Both Are Necessary for a Strong Community

If the only tool you have is a hammer,
then the whole world looks like a nail.
—Mark Twain

Two Tools

Mark Twain's saying reminds us that habit powerfully shapes the way people see problems and work toward solutions. In community problem solving, the habit of relying on programs for solutions can lead people to act like a woodworker whose only tool is a hammer. Imagine how strange it would look to see someone trying to cut wood by smashing it with a hammer, and how much stranger it would be if he said, "This is the only way there is to get this job done." The job would go much better if the woodworker had both a hammer and a saw, and the knowledge to pick the right tool for the job.

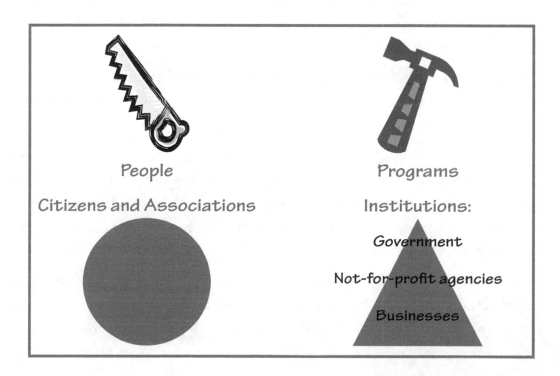

People

Citizens and Associations

Programs

Institutions:

Government

Not-for-profit agencies

Businesses

In community problem solving the two tools, like the hammer and the saw, are citizens and associations –**people**– and institutions of government, non-profits, and business –**programs**. Each tool is valuable in a different way. Clear recognition of their different capacities makes good working partnerships possible. In thoughtfully negotiated partnerships, institutions and citizens each do what they do best.

The habit of counting on programs alone to solve community problems weakens citizens and their associations and dims awareness of the unique contribution that citizens make. The saw gets dull and rusty and people lose the skill to use it.

The Geometry Lesson

Triangles: Institutions and Agencies

Institutions and agencies are one type of tool for community development, one mechanism for getting things done. All institutions have certain common characteristics. I represent them as triangles because they have a hierarchy of authority –a top-to-bottom control structure that can be seen in organization charts shaped like triangles. Institutions have goals to achieve and products to produce: cars, airplane passenger trips, housing units, or counseling sessions. Paid employees implement the institution's agenda. Consumers use their services and buy their products.

Agencies are good community problem solving tools when what's needed is efficiency, reliability, uniformity, expertise, and focus. To make a lot of something standardized in a uniform way, *go to an agency.*

Rigidity vs Flexibility. Agencies' strength is also the source of a dilemma. Efficiency and uniformity can lead to a kind of rigidity and inflexibility that makes it difficult to respond to unique and changing community situations. The desire for sustained production can make institutional survival more important than the organization's stated purpose.

Client vs Citizen. Agencies can create dependency by relating to people as receivers of services that increase agency power, not as producers of results that promote common good. The root of the word client in Latin refers to "a person who is a dependent follower," whereas the origin of the word citizen refers to "a person who acts, united with others." The more of a community's problems are addressed by helping agencies rather than by local residents, the more likely it is that local residents will think like clients waiting for help rather than citizens who act to solve problems. The unintended consequence of professional agency help is that people often grow in dependency on helpers as they are helped.

Circles: Citizens and Their Associations

The tool of citizens and their associations are represented as circles, because they are more consensual in decision making, they come together around what the people involved care about, and the association's members do most of the work. Citizen groups rely much more on unpaid members than on paid staff, they are energized by the relationships and motivation to act that their members share and build up together.

Citizens and associations shine at innovation, invention, and flexibility. Their dilemma is that consensus and fluid response to changing concerns can make association's responses to long-term problems fragile and temporary.

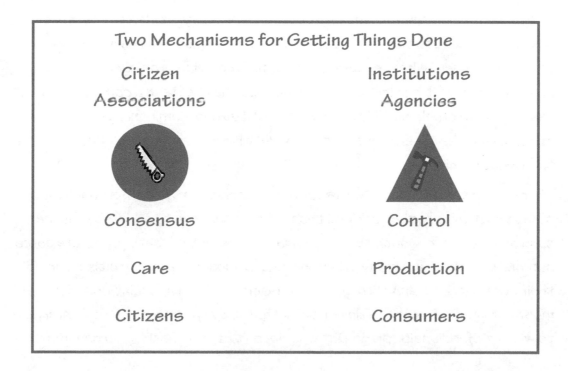

Two Mechanisms for Getting Things Done

Citizen Associations	Institutions Agencies
Consensus	Control
Care	Production
Citizens	Consumers

A New Balance for Community Problem Solving

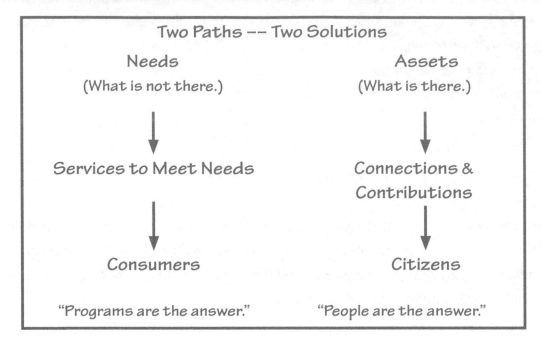

Today, most effort toward community problem solving comes from the action of agencies, government or non-profit. The tremendous capacity of citizens remains on the sidelines. This imbalance of responsibility is caused by following a path that assumes that programs are the primary answer. To follow this path, start with counting-up needs, define community problems in terms of the agency services to meet those needs, and find money to deliver services to the consumers who are waiting for them. Over-reliance on agencies and programs makes it harder to find and mobilize the assets in a community that can help solve problems. This dilemma of institutional dominance over people is often called "the consumer society," a world where what we get defines us more than what we give.

For example, if violence towards youth is a concern, a typical approach measures the degree of the need and then sets up services to address violence, such as classes for youth about staying safe, parent education, or more police patrols. But there are many other things that could be done by citizens in their everyday lives and through their capacity to form associations. However, most community members do not think that they can help much compared to what professionals can do. But who doesn't have something to contribute toward a safer community? A person can contribute to safety without professional knowledge about violence as a social problem. Programs are not the whole story, people are also the answer.

More and more agencies recognize their limits and seek a new balance. A balance in which citizen action and professional service each play their part.

What Is the Effect of Counting on Agencies More than on People?

I have illustrated this idea of programs over people in workshops in many different places by asking a volunteer who holds a triangle representing programs to climb onto a chair so that programs tower over the volunteer who holds the circle representing people and associations. In every group, most participants see this image of institutions reigning over people as an accurate reflection of their home situation. How does this structure affect agencies and citizens?

Professionals who work in agencies typically speak of how overwhelmed they are, trying to do jobs that are nearly impossible because of insufficient resources and energy. People in neighborhoods and communities often express a lack of confidence in their own abilities to solve problems, believing agencies should deliver solutions to them. This structure weakens citizens: unused capacities atrophy.

This is a difficult structure to change. The dynamics at work in this example are common to many different community situations. If a partnership working on better reading outcomes for a school has a membership of 50% educators and 50% parents, the professional points of view and service solutions will dominate unless there is an intentional effort on both sides to strengthen the voice and active contribution of the parents. What accounts for this? It is not that professionals are inherently controlling. In fact, many times professionals want very much for people to participate. But parents often defer to professional knowledge. The staff has been thinking about this meeting all day while the parents were working and dealing with other issues in their lives. The meeting might be at school at a time difficult for parents to participate. The meeting may use educational jargon foreign to parents. You can likely name a dozen other reasons that professionals will tend to be "on the chair" above parents even when trying to get parents more active as participants.

Exercise
Programs Over People

Discuss these three questions in a small group.

- What is the effect on agencies and their staff of being primarily responsible for community problem solving?

- What is the effect on community citizens' groups and community members of not being in charge of community problem solving?

- People often suggest the answer is that agencies get off the chair and be at the same level as citizens and associations? Is this enough?

Reflection: Use this space to record the most important thing you learned from this discussion. How can you act differently as a citizen to keep this programs-over-people structure from taking over?

It is not enough for agencies to say, "Let's be partners". It takes intentional effort to create a space in which citizens can "get on the chair" by assuming responsibility and power.

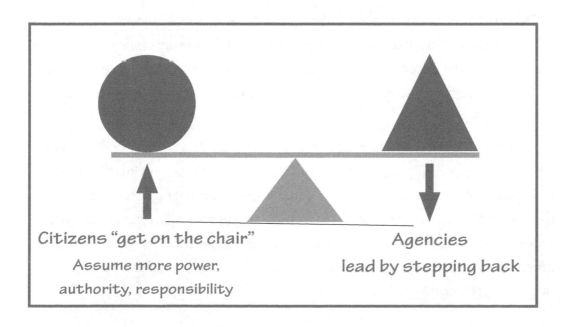

Citizens "get on the chair"

Assume more power, authority, responsibility

Agencies

lead by stepping back

Exercise

Getting Citizens on the Chair

1. What are the factors that make it difficult for agencies to step "off the chair" and for people other than helping professionals to step "on the chair"?

2. What actions will successfully open a space where citizens can choose to "get on the chair" and where agencies can "get off the chair"?

Reflection: Use this space to record what you have learned from this discussion. What actions can you take to increase the responsibilities citizens take?

Agencies Lead by Stepping Back

Communities grow stronger when community and agency leaders work together to create better and better answers to these two questions :

- How can citizens get stronger and more organized?

- How can agencies become better servants of citizens getting stronger?

Citizens become stronger by taking action. Exercise of civic capacity builds civic muscle and overcomes atrophy as people grow in confidence and competence. Agencies become stronger when they learn to "lead by stepping back." This means both offering good services and expanding civic space by investing in citizen efforts.

Partnerships between agencies and citizens must be citizen-centered in order to purposefully overturn the habits that turn citizens into consumers. Real partnership has the power to make decisions and the power to direct money on the table for negotiation. A meaningful portion of authority and resources relocate from agencies to citizens. People will only get involved and contribute when they are truly at the table, sharing in decision making and sharing in the control of resources.

Community Development vs Service Coordination

*"No matter how hard you try to do the wrong thing,
it will not make it the right thing to do."*

—*Old Oklahoma Saying*

If you want applesauce, you need apples; if you want marmalade you need oranges. No matter how hard you try, you cannot make applesauce from oranges. Professionals often act from an agency-centered view of the world and try to mobilize citizens by using an organizational structure designed to coordinate services among agencies. They first set up an organization that brings agency representatives together, and then attempt to engage the wider community in doing the work. This approach does not work very well because citizens are mobilized by relationships, not by agency roles and requirements. It is very difficult for the same partnership structure to handle both service coordination and community development.

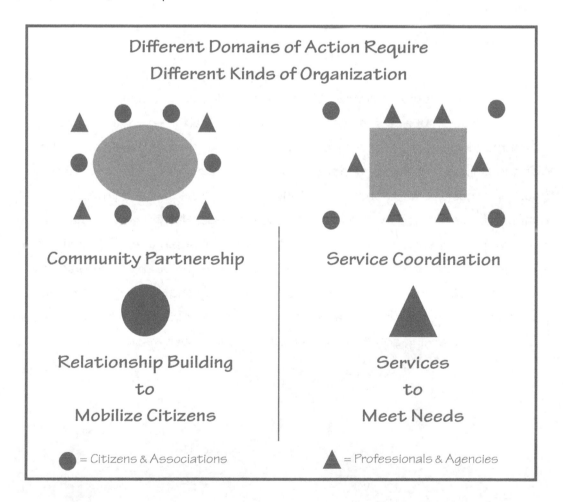

**Different Domains of Action Require
Different Kinds of Organization**

Community Partnership

Service Coordination

**Relationship Building
to
Mobilize Citizens**

**Services
to
Meet Needs**

● = Citizens & Associations   ▲ = Professionals & Agencies

The start determines the finish. A service coordination structure can work well to deal with problems that are best addressed by experts, agencies, and institutions working inside the boundaries of their professional roles. To co-ordinate efforts to assess learning disabilities or find children with reading problems, set up an agency-centered structure. But to involve people from the everyday life of a community, put connector leaders at the center from the very first effort to define the problems that need addressing. To mobilize local business people in expanding employment opportunities for people with dis-abilities, the leadership group must include citizens who have earned trust and influence among a wide circle of local business people.

When agency representatives in a service coordination structure recognize the importance of involving everyday people through their associations, they learn that it works better to set up a new community partnership than to try to bring citizens and associations into the existing service coordination structure.

Creating Citizen Space

A community partnership successfully involves well-connected leaders who use their relationships to bring other groups to join the action. This can only happen in **citizen space**: a place where connector leaders decide the agenda. A community partnership creates an open space where citizens can frame the possibilities for effective action, say "yes" to action, and invite others to act. Willingness to ask others to get involved depends on the strength of a connector leader's motivation to act. A business leader will go to other busi-ness people and say "I want you to join this" only because the effort provides a chance to express shared care. People's ability to persuade others to say 'yes' is limited, even among close friends. That's why the focus of community partnership is centered on what a community cares about, as that caring is expressed in learning conversations that discover motivation to act.

How NOT to Connect People and Programs

Policies and programs reflect our response to the map we create of the world around us. Our map, like all maps, is not the territory it portrays. And it can be a map that inaccurately portrays the territory that surrounds us. We all know of the European map makers who described a flat earth without a western hemisphere. Their inaccurate map shaped the policies, plans and action of mariners, kings, nations and communities.

As we set sail into the twenty-first century, it is appropriate to reexamine the map that is used in most of our current policy-making in order to see whether it will show the way to safe, wise and healthful communities.

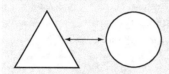 Whenever policy makers happen to recognize that there is a community territory, the map they draw usually looks like the one on the left. This map is commonly described as a **partnership**. It suggests that each is an equal owner of or participant in an activity. However, the recent history of the actual system-community relationships suggests that the real territory is quite different. At least three kinds of alternative relationships are actually present in most cases.

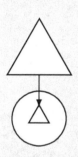 The first alternative is a relationship of the form on the left. In this relationship a subsidiary of a system is located in the community to assure access to local need. This relationship is most accurately described as **system outreach** rather than partnership.

The second form of relationship looks like the form on the right. In this case the community is used as a source of unpaid workers for systems. The accurate name for this relationship is **volunteering** rather than partnership.

 The graphic on the left maps a relationship in which a citizen is chosen by a system to react to a system's plans. The citizen does not have authority or a vote but is advisory. The correct name for this relationship is a **citizen advisory** group rather than a partnership.

A genuine partnership is a relationship of equal power between two parties with distinctive interests. Each preserves its authority, distinct capacity and integrity but gains power through the partnership.

It is difficult to find many examples of authentic partnerships of this nature between systems and associations. Instead, the actual power relationship is most often a system using a community of associations to foster its own ends.

Indeed, the principal history of the twentieth century relationships between systems and associations is the ascent of the system and the decline of the community of associations. The actual map of our era would chart this relationship chronologically in this way:

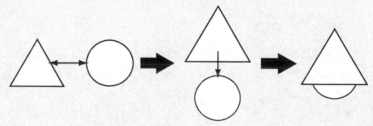

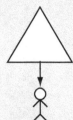

The actual territory is one in which systems have moved from equality to dominance and then have generally eclipsed or pushed out the associations and their functions. This has happened as systems have commanded ever more authority, professional dominance, technology and public and private dollars. Another name for the result of this dominance is a "consumer society". It produces an unprecedented belief system and culture of its own.

Central to this belief system is the proposition that is embodied in the social policy making map with which we began. That map indicates that systems produce our well being. We understand that our health is in a medical system. Our safety is in a criminal justice system. Our security is in a pension system. Our learning is in a school system. Our mental stability is in a mental health system. Our justice is in a lawyer. Our family stability is in a family service system. Our home is in the hands of the Allstate system. Our house is produced by the Caldwell Banker system. And our meals are the product of McDonalds.

When this belief system becomes the dominant social construction of a people, their map of a good society is shown at the right. One way of accurately describing this map is that it is a comprehensive, coordinated, wrap-around, inter-professional, multi-service system.

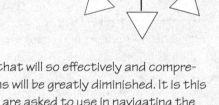

Those policy makers who believe in this map urge that its ability to produce evermore well-being for its clients depends upon two changes:

• More money for the system

• Better administration of the system

The result of these changes will be "systems reform" that will so effectively and comprehensively target clients that our current social problems will be greatly diminished. It is this proposition and the map upon which it is based that we are asked to use in navigating the twenty-first century.

–John McKnight

From: *A 21ˢᵗ Century Map for Healthy Communities and Families*

download from: www.northwestern.edu/ipr/publications/community/century.html

Programs and People: Agencies Can Invest In Both

Can an agency deliver services and successfully engage the wider community? The answer is yes, if agency leaders can stay clear about the different kinds of organizational structures and different practices. each investment requires. An agency must maintain a definite boundary between service delivery and its investments in mobilizing community. This boundary gives each distinct kind of action room to grow. Service delivery starts with a professionally defined answer to address a professionally assessed need. Community mobilizing starts with listening to citizens for the answer to a fundamental question: what do people care enough to act on?

Experience shows that where service delivery and community mobilizing are mixed up, neither activity works very well. Both citizens and professionals need a common language —summarized in this chapter— to describe the difference between delivering services and mobilizing community. Clarity about the different contributions that each activity makes allows establishment of the distinct conditions that each needs to be effective.

Exercise

How Can an Agency Do Both Services and Community Mobilizing?

Discuss these questions in a small group.

* What problems have you encountered when agencies do both service provision and community mobilizing?

* How can one agency successfully support both different activities?

Reflection: Use this space to record the most important things you have learned from discussing the way an agency can support both service delivery and mobilizing community.

Being a Champion for Change

Many years ago I worked on water contamination issues in a small Colorado community called Commerce City, near Denver. State agencies and federal agencies both minimized the problem. Yet residents knew the water was bad in their community. We made little progress until a middle-level Colorado Department of Health manager secretly revealed to us the facts about how badly the water was polluted and how little the state was doing. Without her help to find the facts, which then became the foundation for our campaign, we could never have succeeded. Many a quiet hero makes it possible each day to build local democracy where citizens can act like citizens.

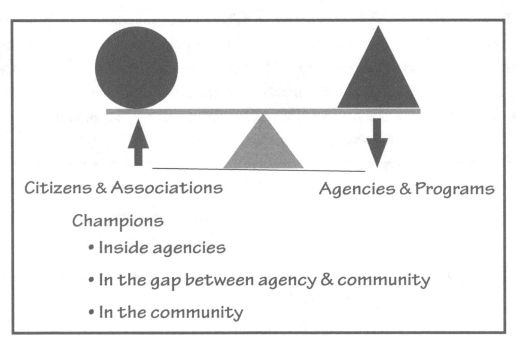

Citizens & Associations   Agencies & Programs

Champions
  • Inside agencies
  • In the gap between agency & community
  • In the community

Ultimately, the possibility of asset based community development can only be realized through the courage, determination, and leadership of champions for re-balancing community action. Only people who are committed to citizens standing on the chair –assuming responsibility and power- and agencies leading by stepping back will make this fundamental shift happen. Champions for change might be paid to work as agency leaders, be staff on the edge of agencies, work between community and agency in the gap, or be community organizers in the neighborhood. What they have in common is the conviction that the future of strong, welcoming communities lies in people acting like citizens who care rather than clients who wait to be serviced.

Regular People Can Do Amazing Things

The Denver Foundation Leads By Supporting Neighborhood Partnerships

Christine Soto

I was apprehensive, but excited, when I was hired in 1997 to implement a neighborhood program at The Denver Foundation. "Inaccessible" and "elitist" were two words that were often used to describe Denver's community foundation when I first became aware of it in the early 1980's. Though I came to realize that these descriptions weren't totally accurate, this was the perception of much of Denver's nonprofit community. Founded in 1925, in the mid 1990s it still had this reputation, a rather small endowment for a 70-plus year old organization, and a board of trustees comprised of "the upper crust."

I came to The Denver Foundation with a 25-year background in direct service and management of nonprofit organizations, primarily with youth development agencies. I had done counseling, raised money, managed volunteers. However, I had never worked in traditional community development..I believe this was an advantage when I became the Program Officer in charge of creating and implementing what eventually became the Strengthening Neighborhoods Program of The Denver Foundation.

Today, this program has earned national acclaim for its grassroots, resident-centered approach to engaging people in improving the neighborhoods they live in. In 2005, it celebrated giving away its one millionth dollar in grants. These grants averaged $3,000 and were made to groups comprised of three or more residents – groups that are not nonprofit organizations. Ask around today, and those in the know about the nonprofit and foundation sector will describe The Denver Foundation as the most connected-to-the-community foundation operating in metro Denver.

How did this once stodgy and exclusive foundation make this transition? And why do it in the first place?

For the Foundation, the "why" was to increase community awareness of the Foundation and to connect it to the community at the grassroots level, where it had no connection. As one wise man said, we were "putting community back into the community foundation." It was also about doing something new – and it did, in fact, usher in a new era of openness, accessibility, innovation

Learn more about Strengthening Neighborhoods at www.denverfoundation.org/

and collaboration for The Denver Foundation. It was also unique: at the time no other foundation in Colorado was making grants to groups of neighbors to improve their neighborhoods.

For me, the "why" was about putting into action my belief that regular people, working together, can do amazing things. I was convinced that by giving people small amounts of money, along with lots of flexibility on how to use that money, they would make things happen in a way that organized philanthropy or formally structured nonprofits or government could not. Hence, one of our first principles: *We shall trust in the people*.

My first assignment was to find out what was happening – or not – in neighborhoods of Denver, and what models already existed in the philanthropic world for working successfully at this level.

My explorations led to many places, but most significantly to the Charles Stewart Mott Foundation and the Asset Based Community Development Institute. In the early 80's, Mott had funded a group of community foundations around the country to begin neighborhood-focused grantmaking. Rainbow Research wrote a series of reports and evaluations about this effort (www.rainbowresearch.org). The group, while no longer getting direct funding from Mott, had continued to share experiences and lessons. Making small grants available to resident groups was one of the tools widely used.

The ABCD Institute had begun to publish its experiences and reflections about how communities, regardless of their challenges, also had innumerable assets. And, if tapped into and supported, those assets could be the key to amazing and positive change.

What I learned from these two sources resonated with what I was learning from a variety of individuals and organizations. It reinforced my own belief that while people had the ability to make enormous change in their environments, they needed to do it together. Another principle: *We shall encourage people to work with one another.*

The first challenge was to get people to apply for these grants. We were interested in giving money to people to do after-school homework clubs, or group art projects, or fixing up elder's homes. I learned that distributing printed information wasn't going to do it – we had to get out there and tell people about it, and convince them that they could get this money.

Through a series of neighborhood meetings, word slowly spread about this foundation that was interested in giving money to people – regular people – to do what they believed would be good for the neighborhood they lived in. By talking to lots of individuals, I would identify a core group of neighborhood residents who were connected

Havey Productions

Christine Soto

to lots of other residents. I would invite them to a meeting at a neighborhood coffee shop and ask them to help me plan a larger neighborhood information meeting. We would serve a free dinner and provide free babysitting. And we would tell them about this free money —money that was available for them to try out their ideas, their dreams. Another principle: **We shall go to where the people are.**

The most common comment I heard at these meetings? "I can't believe The Denver Foundation is here asking us what we want to do." Having lived in the nonprofit world for so many years, I had come to expect people to know about nonprofits and about the foundations that helped to support them. It was obvious that outside the formal nonprofit structure, The Denver Foundation was unknown. Heck, foundations in general were an unknown. This was humbling to all of us, staff and volunteers, and accentuated the importance of reaching out.

How has this changed The Denver Foundation? What were the events, small and large, that moved the Foundation from inaccessible to approachable, from elitist to community-friendly?

- We brought the power structure to the people. Trustees and committee members would attend the neighborhood information meetings, the banker and the utilities company CEO breaking bread with and listening to neighborhood residents. Sharing a meal brings people closer together, and the meetings illustrated the power of listening. I have become a better listener because of this.

- The Strengthening Neighborhoods Committee changed the "face" of the Foundation. It began recruiting residents of the targeted neighborhoods to serve alongside the board of trustee members. Eventually, resident members of the Strengthening Neighborhoods Committee were recruited to be members of the Board of Trustees. As the Board expanded its inclusiveness, these new voices had an impact. In 2003, the Board of Trustees approved the Foundation's first-ever policy on anti-discrimination policies and practices of grantee organizations.

- The diversity and inclusiveness of The Denver Foundation's staff increased as a result of who was hired for Strengthening Neighborhoods. We hired the only bilingual Program Officer in the Foundation's history. An African-American support staff person with family roots in the civil rights movement was promoted to Assistant Program Officer. A Mexican-born immigrant was hired for his community organizing skills and ability to provide hands-on technical assistance to Spanish-speaking residents taking on leadership roles in neighborhoods groups.

- As the staff and the board became more reflective of the racial and ethnic diversity of the community, the Strengthening Neighborhoods program took off. In 2005, the number of grant applications sky-rocketed. Groups of neighbors of all kinds sought us out. Yet another principle : If we look like them, they will come.

- Continually looking for ways to develop neighborhood assets, early in its history, Strengthening Neighborhoods hosted a forum on community organizing, where organizers, and the CEOs of the companies they organized against, came together in a dialogue about neighborhood leadership. As a result, The Strengthening Neighborhoods Initiative made large grants of $25,000 and above, primarily to community organizing groups that impacted multiple neighborhoods.

- In 2000, when reviewing funding priorities for the Community Grants Program, the Foundation's primary grantmaking program, the Board of Trustees unanimously adopted a priority in Civic & Education that reads: Enhance neighborhood assets by involving residents in strengthening their own neighborhoods. Funding of organizations using organizing and advocacy as tools of community change increased in the Community Grants Program. In 2005, The Denver Foundation became one of six funders tapped to be part of the Philanthropic Community Organizing Collaborative, funded by the Ford Foundation.

This is especially amazing when one considers that during the first year I was at the Foundation, the executive director of the largest community organizing entity in Denver told me that he had been given the brush-off just a couple of years earlier. He was told, "The Denver Foundation is just not interested in funding community organizing, so you shouldn't bother applying." Times do change.

This reinvestment in the oh-so-powerful tool of community organizing was invigorating to me. The Strengthening Neighborhoods program was a major force in reshaping the Foundation's financial investments – it was putting power back into the people's hands. It made me realize that, even though it takes time, you can turn the ocean liner around.

As I reflect on the impact of the resident-centered, asset-based work of Strengthening Neighborhoods, I am stunned by the many ways in which this relatively small program has changed the face of The Denver Foundation. The evidence:

- Transparency – openness about how the foundation does things and with whom – is routine

- Being a responsive and accessible community resource is expected

- Listening to the community is now an imperative

- Flexibility and innovation are highly prized

- Diversity and inclusiveness has expanded at the staff level, among Board and other volunteers, and in the types of grantees

- Collaborative efforts are a priority

There is no turning back, for either The Denver Foundation, or for me. The work going forward is about continually broadening the term "community" to include marginalized people of all kinds, to encourage nonprofit institutions to engage the people they serve not as clients but as collaborators, to insist that all non-profits and foundations embrace inclusiveness, and to require foundations to be transparent in all ways.

christinesoto@comcast.net

We shall trust in the people.

We shall encourage people to work with one another.

We shall *go to where the people are.*

An ABCD Community Partnership

- Owned and controlled by local people

- Desired outcome: local people act as productive citizens vs local people receive services

- A community organization that engages the wider community as an engine for ABCD.

- Seeks resources both inside and outside the community

- Both cooperative and challenging; building connections among people and groups and at times challenging institutions for social change.

- Broad participation—every member of the community has gifts to offer, not just designated leaders

- Inclusive—there is no one whose gifts are not needed.

V

Organizing an ABCD Community Partnership

What is an ABCD community partnership?

A group of parents form a group to develop youth jobs in partnership with local businesses. Neighbors organize to influence the city government to provide more recreation services. A group of congregations develop a learning exchange that connects people who want to teach and learn such things as guitar playing, gardening, or computer skills.

Each of these efforts began in the same way: a circle of well-connected local people formed a community partnership. This partnership worked together towards a purpose that involved their community in action. In this kind of partnership –sometimes called a community organization–most members are everyday citizens, not the staff of helping agencies. Local citizens and their associations are at the center of decision-making and are the principal producers of outcomes. A community partnership is the most powerful vehicle for mobilizing the community. This chapter outlines the community organizing steps that build a citizen-centered community partnership.

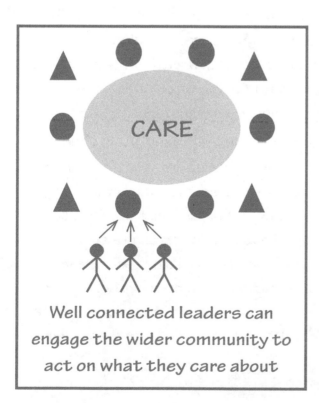

Well connected leaders can engage the wider community to act on what they care about

Community Organizing

Community organizing brings together people and groups in a community to act on what they care about. Organizing may build a growing circle of people who take collective action —like the partnership that developed youth jobs did— or a network connecting diverse people —like the partnership that created the learning exchange did. Historically, community organizing in the United States has brought together people without power so they have a voice in decision making to influence local institutions. The battle has been to get a seat at the table of power for those usually left out. In addition to improving the accountability of business and government, community organizing has also developed local partnerships that act for other purposes such as mutual aid, economic development, and inclusion of marginalized people.

When people who differ in many obvious ways learn about what is truly important to each other, a connection often emerges in which the learners find common purpose. We differ in a thousand ways; age, size, ethnicity, race, religion, belief, history. And yet the more we dwell on what is most important to us, the more we discover what we care about in common. For example, most everyone has similar dreams, fears, and hopes about their children's future. When we share dreams about our children, a common ground emerges that unites us and moves us. ABCD organizing seeks this source of energy, which is activated by expressing and acting on shared meaning. Conversation starts the energy moving towards more relationships and more meaningful action.

Think of organizing as moving repeatedly through a circle of three interacting activities: conversations to discover what people care about, meaningful action upon what people care about, and the connections that grow among people who act together. This circle of conversation, action, and connection is a community development structure that can widen through a community like the ripples from a pebble dropped in a pond. Human beings seek meaning naturally, and organizing is a process to lead people to meaning. Energy and life reside in this circle of meaningful conversation, action, and relationship. These three activities are different manifestations of the same inner reality, the beating heart of community.

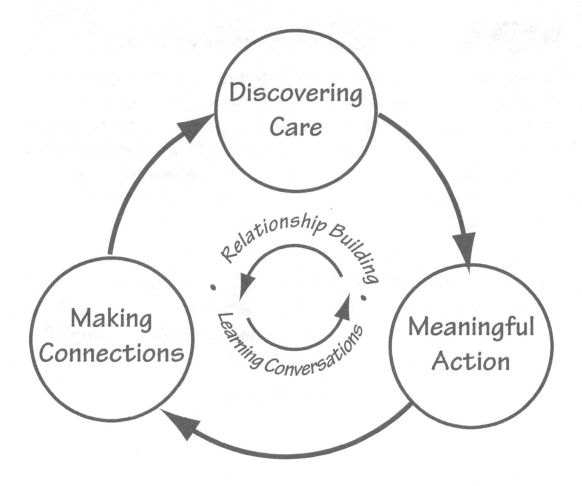

An ABCD connector-leaders group includes people with connections who are residents, local association or congregation leaders, or local business leaders. This group is made up of people who live, associate, or worship in the community. It functions with assistance from supporters from government, business, and human services who lead by stepping back. The connector-leaders group follows the principle: "Never to do anything that nobody wants", and sets its agenda by listening to what citizens care enough to act on. The goal is not service delivery but activating the productive capacity of the local community. The leaders of an ABCD community partnership act from the heartfelt conviction that everyone has gifts that the community needs in order to be strong.

Steps to organize an ABCD Community Partnership

There are typically six steps in forming a strong ABCD community partnership group. Through these steps, the cycle of organizing activities —making connections, discovering care, meaningful action— ripples out from an initiating group to a connector-leader's group and on to an ABCD community partnership group. Each cycle engages a wider and wider circle of citizens and associations in strengthening their community. These steps are...

1. Initiating group begins work
2. Hire and develop an ABCD community organizer
3. Start learning conversations to build connector-leaders group
4. Discover a good issue through learning conversations
5. Develop a community partnership of well connected people to act on the issue
6. Find and mobilize assets to address issues

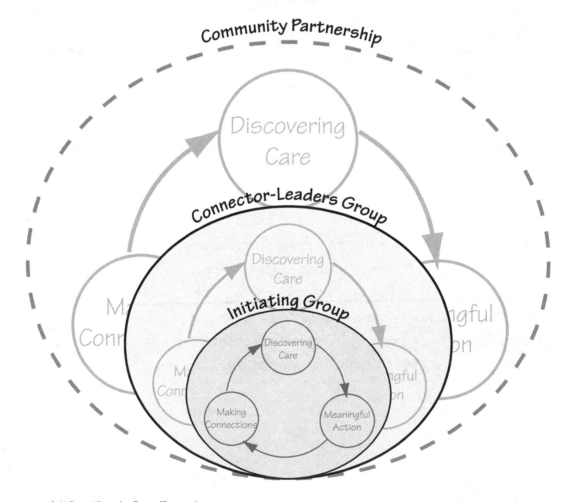

The Initiating Group

This group includes individuals and representatives of institutions, associations, and congregations who want to invest in and support the formation of a citizen centered community partnership. The initiating group may provide funding, be a fiscal agent, build support, and clear away barriers to the forming of the connector-leaders organizing group. This getting started group may continue after the community partnership is formed as an allies group of well connected people who can open doors and enroll new partners for the ABCD organizing group. The initiating group hires the community organizer and directs the organizer until the leaders group of the community partnership forms to take over this role.

Exercise

The Initiating Group

Discuss these three questions in a small group:

1. What could you see this group doing in your community?
2. What kind of local people and groups could be valuable as members of this group?
3. Who do you know that is the kind of person needed for a "getting started" group?

Reflection Use this space to record what you have learned from discussing the Initiating Group. What is most important to remember about the forming and functioning of this group?

Hire and develop an ABCD community organizer

The gifts of the ABCD organizer.

Community organizers are the paid staff of a community partnership. The organizer assists in forming a leaders group of well-connected people and then helps this group bring community members into relationship for action. They work to get citizens to step up "on the chair" to take effective action. Good organizers are both good listeners and good persuaders. They can listen to discover what citizens care enough act on, and then get people to recognize that they themselves can act effectively to address what matters to them. Organizers are both encouraging and challenging, helping citizens grow in confidence and competence. Good organizers believe in their community. They enjoy teaching and are willing to build relationships in which they can be influential

> **Community organizers are about getting other people to do it.**
>
> **–John McKnight**

without a position of formal authority over those they organize. They like the challenge of being self-disciplined and self-directing.

Organizers assist in forming a group of leaders who then take charge of the organizers, including their hiring and firing.

ABCD organizers focus on engaging the gifts of every community member. They challenge and encourage the leadership group to keep reaching out to bring in the assets and energies of people who are often left out.

The test of an organizer is the empowerment of a wider and wider partnership of citizens and associations. Leadership, connection, participation, and results grow as people continue to act from care and relationship. In contrast, activists or advocates measure themselves in terms of what they themselves have done for the people and causes they represent.

The organizer's bottom line is the number of citizens and associations who say, "Yes" to participation, and "Yes" to action. This means being assertive in seeking people out and asking for their participation in action. It also means being willing to hear "no" and go forward anyway. A good organizer is like my father, a great salesman who always believed the customer was around the next corner. Once he sold a building in a market where experts discouraged him from looking for buyers. My father said, "I don't care about all those people who don't want to buy it. I just need to find that one person who will buy it!" And he did. Good organizers have that kind of determination and relish the struggle with difficult situations.

Good organizers come from many walks of life. There is much they need to learn but no particular curriculum that prepares them. They share a genuine liking for and belief in people, a taste for the rough and tumble of community life, and a passion for mobilizing citizens to take meaningful action. They work hard to develop their organizing gifts.

Qualities To Look For In An ABCD Community Organizer

- Relationship builder, connector

- Good salesperson

- Not <u>the</u> leader but good at getting other people to act

- Teacher

- Critical thinker

- Seeks potential & relentlessly sees "glass half full"

- Tough-minded and disciplined

- Can be challenging AND supporting

Exercise

Gifts of a Good ABCD Organizer?

Discuss these questions in a small group.

1. Who do you know who is good at getting other people to act?

2. What is he or she like?

3. What do you think will help support and develop an organizer like the person you know who can activate others?

Reflection Use this space to summarize what you have learned from this discussion. What will you look for in an organizer? How will you support people to develop their gifts for organizing?

───────────────────────────────

Paid organizers and unpaid citizen leaders.

Almost every effective community partnership has a paid organizer. Citizen leaders are simply too busy with life demands to dedicate themselves to meaningful action without some staff support. Considering how busy effective people are today the maxim that "organizers can work themselves out of a job" has become little more than a myth. Citizen leaders –people who have a following among other citizens who trust them– contribute their wisdom about their community to indicate where meaningful action will make the most difference, their connections and credibility to involve others, and their energy to move care into action. Organizers follow the direction indicated by these leaders and dedicate their paid time to assembling and servicing the organization that provides a vehicle for asset based community development.

Sometimes institutions want to pay citizens to act like citizens. They offer money to those who come to community planning. This is always a mistake. It confuses the exchange of money with the exchange of care that is the citizens gift. It is encouraging to support participation with a wonderful meal, free childcare, or transportation. It is demeaning to pay someone for acting as a citizen.

Learning to be an organizer.

Organizing is an art that integrates many practices. It is not a set of simple techniques that can be learned in a classroom or from a book (even this one). Organizers learn through practice and reflection on practice. Consultation and training with people who are more experienced guides the cycle of action and reflection that develops the knowledge and skills that allow organizers the full and effective use of their gifts. A community partnership's budget needs more than just an item for the organizer's salary, It also needs an allocation for consultation to the organizer and for the organizer's participation in learning experiences.

A **learning circle** of people who commit themselves to meet regularly with an organizer, listen carefully to the organizer's account of his or her work, and support the organizer in learning through reflection. This is a powerful resource to complement and give grounding to what an organizer learns from consultation and training. The questions that guide a learning circle are straightforward:

1. What is working?
2. What are the highest possibilities in the situation right now?
3. What will it take to mobilize action toward those highest possibilities?
4. What are the most important lessons in what is happening now?

The highest purpose of evaluation is learning not monitoring and the most effective form of assessment is guided self assessment. The five standards on the following page offer a structure that helps an organizer avoid distractions and the trap of working very hard but achieving little.

Quality Standards For Organizers

Doing Learning Conversations. How many learning conversations did you do this week? If as a full time organizer you do not do 15-20 learning conversations per week (30-60 minutes each), then you are not primarily organizing but doing something else. What you are doing might be good, but it will not organize your community. Organizing requires relationship building through learning conversations. These opportunities to listen are the way you prepare the ground in your community for participation, organization, and meaningful action.

Leaders and Members Growing Participation. At the beginning of a local initiative, the organizer's goal is to develop the connector-leader group at the center of the community partnership. Is this group growing week by week? What evidence do you have that the connector-leader group is having productive meetings? Later the focus shifts to expanding the membership of people actively participating and contributing to the community through the community partnership's work. Does the diversity of the people active through the community partnership reflect the diversity of the whole community? What evidence do you have that the group is growing in its ability to help people experience diversity as a source of strength, not a problem or a matter for awkwardness. Can the community partnership honestly say that it is weaving a tapestry of many different threads?

Inviting the Contribution of Marginalized People. Are a growing number of people who might ordinarily not be seen as having gifts actively included in your work as contributors? Are you involving young people? The elderly? People with disabilities? People on welfare? Is the conviction growing among your group and in the community that everyone has something to offer?

Setting a Citizen-Centered Agenda. Is the action agenda of the community partnership coming from the connector-leaders group rather than from the management of government, human service, or granting agencies? Is the action agenda arising from listening in the community through many conversations and meetings? Is there evidence of a constituency for action on the issues chosen? Is your community partnership doing what people in the community want to do rather than doing what someone else thinks they need to do?

Getting Results. Are you accomplishing anything or just talking or just caught up in activity? What evidence do you have that the community partnership is growing increasingly effective at reaching out to new members, planning, setting goals, doing research, finding assets, making connections, and producing results on issues? Are you making new partners? Is the community partnership successful on issues? How would you, as the organizer, describe your contribution to the community partnership's effectiveness?

Build through learning conversations

Learning conversations are the fundamental act of community organizing. Full time organizers usually do 15-20 such conversations per week. Connector-leaders also practice this form of intentional listening and connecting. Bringing people into meaningful conversations begins movement across the threshold from passivity to citizenship. First among the connector-leaders who are at the center of the community partnership, then among widening circles of diverse citizens, people seek to discover what they care about enough to act. Reflecting on the results of many learning conversations forms a picture of what citizens find compelling and what assets are available to the community. This shared sense of concerns and assets allows the connector-leaders group to frame an issue that will mobilize the community.

Learning conversation goals

A learning conversation is an opportunity to build a relationship by seeking to discover motivation to act: the care that generates connection and action. Each citizen has personal motivations to act and each citizen association or congregation has shared motivations to act. What an association cares about at a particular moment may or may not be captured in its official mission statement –in many associations, formal statements may not have caught up with members' developing concerns and purposes. The listener works first to understand what the person or association cares about enough to act. Then the listener asks him or herself…

- How does this person's or association's motivation to act weave them into the tapestry of our community partnership?

- What assets could they bring?

- Who else shares or compliments what they care about enough to act?

LEARNING CONVERSATION GOALS

- Develop a stronger relationship

- Discover motivation to act

- Explore mutual interest & clarify possible action steps

- Find more prospects

Elements of a learning conversation

Opportunities for good learning conversations grow like strawberry vines. The first conversations among members of the connector-leader's group builds an initial list of prospects that grows as those who converse identify others who care about some aspect of the group's organizing interest. A good prospect for early learning conversations will be a leader (someone who has a following) in an association (which already gathers and supports capacity to act) who demonstrates motivation to act and has a potential interest in common with the ABCD community partnership.

Good manners make for good learning conversations. Meet people at times and in places that are comfortable and convenient, Be on time and take no more than the 30-60 minutes the person agreed to. Treat people respectfully and listen carefully.

Conduct the conversation singly or in a pair of inquirers. After several learning conversations, gather with other interviewers to share, summarize, reflect on what you are learning, and revise the process if necessary.

Effective learning conversations begin with clear answers to two important questions:

1. **Who are we?** A good answer to this question establishes your credentials as a representative of a group worth taking seriously. It avoids the person who asks for the learning conversation being perceived as "somebody nobody sent."

    "We're from ABCD Organizing, a group of eleven neighborhood associations who are working together to develop good jobs for youth in our community. Your pastor, Rev Smith suggested that we meet with you."

2. **Why are we meeting with you?** This is a simple direct statement of the interest that brings your group together. The connector-leaders group works out the core of this statement and everyone who has a learning conversation on behalf of the group starts with the same statement of purpose. This sends a message throughout the community that this group is organizing around this issue. The purpose statement raises a question of concern to the community and leaves the person room to express her or his concerns and ideas. It does not try to sell an answer.

"We are working together to create good jobs for young people in our community. We want to hear your thoughts on the issue and see what you think of the ideas we've had so far."

After answering these two questions, the learning conversation proceeds.

3. **Introduction.** This allows a warm-up so that those in the conversation can acknowledge the relationship they have or recognize common interests or connections.

4. **Identify motivation to act**. This question -what do you care about enough to act– is the heart of the learning conversation, It invites the person to talk about motivation to act. Discover as much as possible about the person's concerns, dreams, and gifts. A good conversation lets the person talk about overall motivation to act as well as the specific concerns, dreams and gifts that link the person to the community partnerships' purpose. It may help to have a test question such as, *"Would you want to introduce a young person to your work?"*

5. **Invite next steps**. This question –what do you want to do?– offers the person a connection to the ABCD community partnership. Some people will be ready to take action based on the learning conversation. It's important to offer a next step that they can take to become more involved. It may be a meeting of people who share an interest in some aspect of the issue, for example, the people who care about how congregations can help create youth jobs. It may be an invitation to join in publicity or research activities.

6. **Seek others.** Who else should we invite for learning conversations. This question –who else do you know that might work with us?– continues to grow the network.

After talking to a few people, connector-leaders gather to assess how the conversations are going, talk about any problems, revise the questions based on responses, and discuss what's been found –both people to involve and issues people think are important for action.

1-1 Learning Conversation Notes (Example)

Name   Date

Address

Phone   e-mail   Fax

Occupation

Who suggested the contact?

1. Gifts, capacities, & skills to contribute?

2. Issues and concerns you want to work on?

3. What about (issue of concern to the ABCD community partnership)? Concerns? What should we do that you would work on?

4. Strong relationships with others (associations and institutions)

5. Possible roles in ABCD community partnership?

6. Further contacts for us to see (name and phone)?

Discover a good organizing issue through learning conversations

The connector-leaders group extends and develops the community partnership by mobilizing people and associations around specific issues that citizens care about enough to act. Learning conversations reveal dreams and visions for the community's future as well as problems and concerns. The connector-leader group considers what citizens have said in learning conversations and frames an issue that has these qualities:

1. The issue is **concrete**. People will know when they have succeeded.

2. The issue is **winnable**. There is a reasonable chance of success.

3. The issue is **immediate**. Learning conversations show that there are a number of people who will act on this issue. A meeting that brings together people who have expressed a willingness to act and asks for their commitment to a definite course of action tests the strength of the constituency. Beginning with an issue that is easiest to win usually builds momentum.

4. Action on this issue will **build the community partnership**. Working together will both strengthen the connections among people and bring in new people and associations.

5. Action on this issue has **two tracks**. Working on this issue will mobilize assets within the community and engage assets outside the community.

Organize a community partnership to act on the issue

The connector-leaders group embodies the truth that power is in relationships. This group of 5-15 people who are well connected, have a following in diverse sectors of community life, and have discovered common ground for action, use their relationships to mobilize the community to address a critical, winnable issue. They begin by asking themselves these questions in order to create a list of prospects.

1. Which sectors of our community do we want to involve (for example, business, religious congregations, parents, or specific neighborhoods)?

2. Whom do we know in the sectors of the community we want to involve?

3. Who should make the invitation? Who is best connected to the person or association we want to enroll?

4. What motivation to act could this person or association have?

5. How is our work an opportunity for this person or association to act on what they care about?

6. Whom do we need to get to know that we don't know now?

7. Who do we know that knows the people that we need to get to know?

Once a good issue is identified and the connector-leaders group has begun to reach out and engage people and associations, the community partnership does action research to get a clear picture of the present situation and possible solutions, maps and mobilizes assets to get results, evaluates and celebrates, and then moves on to build even greater citizen power and leadership.

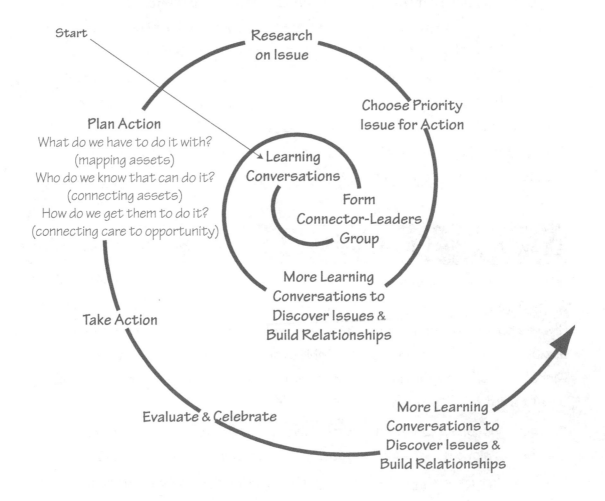

ABCD Reflections from a Dedicated Triangle Shape Shifter

Dan Duncan

As a human services professional and social worker, I have always asked the question; *as a professional what is the best work I can do to help improve the lives of children, families and seniors?*

To answer this question I have developed four principles to help guide my work

- People should always be treated as resources not just recipients or objects of service

- Everyone has gifts

- All truly effective strategies must include a place-based, neighborhood development component

- All good work starts by asking people to share their gifts not by asking them what services they want

Since my early childhood, I have always looked for ways to improve things; the status quo was, and is, never good enough. In addition, coming of age in the 60s with the Viet Nam war, Kent State, and Watergate, I learned the institutional world is not always right.

During my junior year of college, I had the wonderful opportunity to participate in a new program, University Year for Action, a VISTA program for college students. I spent my junior year of college in the inner city of Omaha working with kids as a teacher and with welfare mothers as a National Welfare Rights (NWRO) organizer. Through this experience I began to see the power of neighborhood and citizen centered organizing in the lives of the children and families and the amazing gifts of the mothers other's labeled as "lazy welfare queens". In my senior year, I experienced the life of an Alinsky organizer in the public housing projects in south Omaha. There I helped the residents share their gifts to work together to develop a childcare co-op as well as other self-help activities.

While I experienced the power of citizens and neighborhoods and the negative impact of institutions and professionals, I elected to take the path of becoming a social worker to work from within to change the system. I started social work graduate school with a healthy sense of skepticism as to the promise of services and throughout my graduate education challenged many of the professors and what they were teaching. As part of my commitment to institutional change I created my own nontraditional field placement, with another questioning student, as interns with the Tucson City Manager's office of inter-governmental affairs. At the city we worked as lobbyists for the city and helped develop a plan for intercity neighborhood development.

It should be noted that in 1996 I returned to the School of Social Work as an adjunct professor where I have taught social policy and community and organizational change from an ABCD perspective. Doing my part to respond to my earlier skepticism for a new generation of students.

Dan Duncan

Upon receiving my Masters of Social Work, I helped launch and served as the first director of a centralized food bank. The primary reason we started the food bank was not to hand out food, but to improve the human services delivery system that saw food as an end rather than a means to greater self-sufficiency. From there I moved on to serve as the director of another local nonprofit, before beginning my United Way career. The primary reason I was interested in becoming a United Way professional was to help change the system. I felt working at a major social planning and fund-ing agency would give me the best platform to help the system move from treating individuals as clients and objects of service to resources.

As a United Way professional one of the strategies, I am most proud of, has been to help three United Way's broaden our work from just giving grants to local non-profits and counting "clients" served to providing small grants to formal or informal neighborhood associations or in many instances grants to small groups of residents to help them implement a good idea for their neighborhood. Here at the United Way of Tucson and Southern Arizona the vehicle for our neighborhood grant process is PRO Neighborhoods. PRO is not just another nonprofit, it is a partnership between the City of Tucson, Pima County, the Community Foundation for Southern Arizona and the United Way. PRO was founded about twelve years ago, on the principles of ABCD, following a visit to Tucson by John McKnight. Since its birth, PRO has pro-vided over $500,000 in small grants ($5,000 or less), and thousands of hours of technical assistance and training to help neighborhoods unlock the gifts of their residents. As I think of PRO and its small grants, I view the grants as a giant magnet hovering over the neighborhoods of our city. The magnet attracts potential neighbor-hood leaders who have a good idea to work with some of their neighbors to make the idea a reality. It really is not about the money to fund a project; it is about using the money to unlock the power of the neighborhood and its residents. Again, the key to

PRO Neighborhoods is that it provides the major instituions in our community an opportunity to support citizen centered organizing and not just fund services.

About 12 years ago, I had for a professional dedicated to this work the greatest honor, the opportunity to join the ABCD Institute as an adjunct faculty member. As a faculty member, I have had the privilege to work with John McKnight, Jody Kretzmann, Mike Green and Henry Moore, and all of the other faculty members. Some of the most amazing observers, thinkers, and pioneers working today to improve the human condition, by focusing on what we already have, not what we don't. They have all helped guide my work as a human service professional (a triangle) to always ask the right question: What is the right tool for the job; citizens and neighborhoods caring or professionals and agencies delivering services.

Over my 30 plus years as a human services professional I have tried to never forget the lessons we learn and the results we can achieve when we focus on what people can do, not what they can't do, the power of neighborhoods as the backbone of effective work, and the power of asking people to get involved and share their gifts.

www.proneighborhoods.org

Miss Mary's Walkers

Miss Mary died April 2, 2006 at the age of 98. For thirty-three years, since her retirement, she got up every morning at 5:30 AM and started walking at 6:00 AM. She walked around the Baldwin Park neighborhood for about an hour with four women and one man.

What do you think they were doing while they were walking for that hour? They were talking. They talked about everybody and everything. They also picked up paper. (But Miss Ann, one of the walkers, said, "I pick up paper but I don't do napkins or Kleenex!") Sigmund picked up aluminum cans and put them in a plastic bag and gave them to a guy who supplemented his income selling recycled cans. The walkers also picked up people's newspapers off the sidewalk or the lawn and threw them onto their porches. For this hour everyday that it didn't rain, they studied the neighborhood in every way you can imagine.

Frequently, they'd solve a community problem. For example, when they discovered that some children had knocked out the streetlights in Baldwin Circle. Mary nagged until some of the walkers talked to the children's parents and got restitution.

The walkers tried to figure out what they could do about problems they observed on their daily walks. If they couldn't solve a problem themselves, they identified which local authority they could call to resolve the issue.

What kind of community development group is this? They have no registered name, no tax-exemption, no bank account, no officers or board of directors, no annual general meeting, no membership dues or cards. They are anonymous, but they create benefits: the walkers take steps that help the community stay healthy. They keep the news moving around the neighborhood. They clean-up and recycle as they walk. They identify problems, take action and urge others to take action on neighborhood problems.

As we think about community-building, it seems important that we remember these invisible groups. We should figure out how to lift up their everyday community work, and give them a meaningful role in making the community a better place to live.

– Henry Moore

VI
From Mapping to Mobilizing

You can't connect with what you can't see. The more assets you can see in your community, the more connections you can make in order to build a stronger, richer community life. Asset mapping guides relationship building. It steers a community partnership on the voyage to accomplish its goals by identifying the people, associations, and local institutions of business, service and government whose energies can be linked to the community partnership's. As the number and diversity of connections grow, the power of the community partnership grows.

Some people confuse asset mapping with data collection. They think that the process is over when they have compiled a list of what is out there. This confusion robs the process of its power. Words on a list have no power; relationships around a common purpose have power.

The point of asset mapping is to create relationships that mobilize a community's assets for productive action. These relationships grow when leaders locate assets, identify potential contributions and motivations to act, and then find a way to invite contributions that makes sense from the contributor's point of view. Almost every person and association in a community has something to offer. The limits are mainly limits in the imagination and outreach of connector-leaders and organizers.

Getting Started

An asset map grows as people systematically consider what is there to work with in their community. Mapping begins with a clear statement of what the community partnership wants to accomplish. What concerns does the community partnership want to address, what dreams does it want to realize, what gifts does it want to channel for the common good?

Once purpose becomes clear, asset mappers can identify people to involve and people who can provide the best link to them. Learning conversations that focus people's attention on assets and their mobilization are the most direct route to a live asset map. Directories and websites and library resources can point toward people to engage. Pencil and paper surveys can indicate some local opinions. But these kinds of information are just hints. A real assets map portrays what local people, associations, and institutions are motivated to do and what they have to invest in a common purpose.

Some people worry about analyzing the information they collect. By keeping the inquiry simple and direct, and by relying mostly on learning conversations, the connector-leaders group will be able to make sense of the information they are collecting as it becomes available to them. Each version of the assets map can lead on to another as connector-leaders reflect on what they can see so far, raise better questions, and reach out to more people.

This boot-strapping approach to making an assets map encourages people to begin action as soon as people want to make a contribution rather than waiting for a complete picture to develop.

Here is one example of an effective way to begin mapping associations that might invest in a community partnership's purpose.

1. Get together a meeting of 10 well-connected people in your community who buy the idea of ABCD and care about the community partnership's purpose

2. List the local associations in which these 10 people participate. Describe the nature of the person's connection to each association and put the person's name next to the association.

3. Identify the leaders of each association on the list. A leader in an association is someone with trust and influence in the association.

4. Expand the list to other associations by asking the group to identify community associations that they know about but do not themselves participate in. List the leaders of each and name the members of the group who have a connection to each leader.

5. Cluster the associations on the list by type (for example, service, church, men's, women's, recreation, self-help, etc.).

6. Which of the identified associations are most likely to work on your purpose?

Types of Assets to Map

Individual Asset Inventories:

Gifts, talents, dreams, hopes, fears

Associational Mapping:

Associations you know

Associations you don't know

What do they currently do?

What have they talked about doing but haven't done yet?

What might they do if they were asked?

Institutional Mapping:

Gifts of employees & volunteers

Physical space & equipment

How money is spent —supplies, services, hiring, etc.

Current relationship with community

Dilemmas

Possibilities

Physical Space Mapping:

<u>What is in the neighborhood</u>? Parks, schools, libraries, community centers, hospitals and clinics, apartments, single family homes, neighborhood businesses, bike and walking paths, green spaces, vacant lots, etc.

<u>What happens where?</u> Block club activity, recreation/sports, crime, senior activities, youth activities, clean-ups, code problems, housing type, etc.

Neighborhood Economy Mapping:

How money flows in (and out) of the neighborhood

Neighborhood business development

Opportunities for new businesses

Job opportunities

Once this association map identifies possible assets, the next step is to mobilize them for the community partnership's purpose. For associations, as for individuals and institutions, success in enlisting assets depends on three things:

- Can the association and its leaders see a clear connection between what they care about enough to act on and the community partnership's purpose?
- How strong are the relationships tying the community partnership and its connector-leaders to the association and its leaders?
- Is there an opportunity to contribute that makes sense to the association and its leader. This goes beyond a sense of common interest to a clear specification of the way the association can invest in the community partnership's effort.

Motivation to Act

Why is involvement with you good for them? Every individual or group has a sense of **self-interest** guiding their attention and their decisions about what is important enough to act on. Any reasonably healthy person or organization acts intentionally rather than randomly. Having a good sense of self-interest is not about selfishness or greed. It is about being aware of what contributes to or takes away from well-being. A person asks, "Is this good for me?" An association, school, church, or business asks itself, "Will this action make us stronger?"

Asset mapping begins by identifying a person or a group with potential to contribute to the community partnership's work. This first step leads to learning conversations with the person or the group's leadership. These conversations build personal connections and knowledge of how the person or group will evaluate the invitation to join the community partnership.

Associations

Whether it is called care, motivation to act or self-interest, listening to an association's leaders reveals it. A learning conversation to discover an association's motivation to act explores these questions:

Learning Conversation with an Association Leader (Example)

Introduce yourself, your group and your purpose.

> *We are the parents association of PS 112, seeking to involve local associations in improving literacy in our community.*

Learn about...

- The association—Name, address, telephone, contact person
- Their meetings—Time, date, place, open or by invitation
- Their leaders—Who are they? What do they each do?
- Their primary purpose—What does their association do? Why do they do it?
- What else do they do?
- What might they do in the future? Why might they do it?
- Interest in our purpose?

> *Many people read poorly in our community. Local associations are working together to raise literacy here. Do you think your association or some of your members might be interested in working on this issue with us?*

- If interested, what are next steps?

    How to involve your membership?

    How do we find out what your association might want to do?

- What other local associations are you connected to?
- Do you think any others might be interested in our purpose?

    Who do you know personally?

    Would you introduce us?

- Who else should we get to know?

- What is the present purpose of the association?
- What dilemmas does the association face?
- What are future goals and dreams of the association?
- How might the association be able to contribute to your purpose?
- How might the association want to contribute to your purpose?

Listen deeply. Many association leaders are so busy that they have had little time to go beneath the surface of these questions. If the learning conversation can allow association leaders to enter a dialogue about purpose and vision, a living sense of a meaningful future can take shape. When this dream of a positive future becomes more visible through dialogue, renewed power to act emerges. Those involved in a dialogue that explores purpose and vision often forge a strong connection.

Every association has governing ideals that give meaning to what its members do. Often these ideals are only barely visible in the action the group takes. In learning conversations you are trying to **listen between the words** for the deeper present reality and possible futures. Dreams, visions, and ideals are revealed by *deep asking* and by listening among people in conversation, not through surveys or reading mission statements. To understand the motivation of an association, you must make time for these conversations.

Exercise

Discovering an Association's Self-Interest

In a group of three, explore the self-interest of an association in which one of you is a leader or member. This could be a club, a volunteer group, or a congregation. For 20 minutes, seek to make visible what is really important about this group's self-interest in terms of present purpose, present dilemmas, and future possible purpose. For example a choir might sing, volunteer at a local nursing home, and have considered tutoring kids in the future. They might see tutoring as a way to get future new members.

Reflection. Use this space to record the main things you want to remember about listening for self-interest. What worked well in this discussion to get a deeper sense of the association's motivation to act?

Comment People will usually get a clear picture of the motivation of a group through this kind of conversation with a group leader. Leaders generally know what is important and whether your purpose might fit with their group's purpose. They will also know how to successfully approach their group. This process is essentially the same whether you talk with an individual, an associational leader, or an institutional leader.

Institutional Self-Interest

Every institution –business, nonprofit, or government– has a mission to fulfill. Good managers are guardians of the institution's resources. As guardians they evaluate whether involvement with an outside group brings new strength or takes away strength. If a community partnership wants to move an institution to invest its money, materials, or worker's time and skills, that invitation has to be made based on a good understanding of the institutions sense of what will make it stronger.

The invitation won't work unless it is framed from the institution's point of view. The community partnership needs to know why the institution's managers and workers would see accepting this invitation as strengthening them in ways that it is important to them to be strong. This kind of understanding is especially important when the community partnership is asking for something that will move the institution and its workers outside their typical routines.

Learning conversations with managers and workers allow the community partnership to make powerful invitations. As with associations, the deeper the listening in these learning conversations, the stronger the results.

Congregations: Both Associations and Institutions

Religious congregations are a particularly valuable kind of association for three reasons: many of their members act out of strong values; they endure; and, they usually have some staff to support their activities. A congregation is an association that has some features of an institution, such as a paid staff, a building, and a budget for services offered. A congregation can also be thought of as an "association of associations." For example, every large congregation has many organized groups (such as choir, youth, women's, men's, and prayer groups) that could possibly have distinct assets to engage.Congregations are often strong associations with much promise for community building partnership, as long as congregational leaders can clearly see how a partnership fulfills their purpose and strengthens their congregation.

Find and activate relationship networks

All communities are filled with care —an asset waiting to be made visible— and every community is a web of relationship networks based on trust and influence which are not very visible until you look for them.

To map relationship networks, start with whom you know. Meet with them. Ask them whom they know. Meet with them. Do not do cold calls. Meet with people you are sent to meet.

It isn't practical to have a learning conversation with everyone in an association, congregation, or institution, so look for the leaders, people who have a position of trust, responsibility, and influence in the group. These leaders know the capacities and the dilemmas in their groups and have pretty good ideas about whether the group will want to act with you, what it might want to offer, and how to get its members more involved with you. They know the group's politics: who needs to buy a new idea, who has influence, how to build support, and how to deal with opposition.

Sometimes a group refuses get involved for reasons that are not clear to an outsider. If a group says, "we don't have time for this," it could be that Charlie was the only member opposed but no one else wanted to be involved strongly enough to have a conflict with Charlie. An insider's view of this would lead to a different approach, perhaps starting with a learning conversation with Charlie to discover his viewpoint and make a personal connection.

Exercise

Relationship Networks

Working in threes, give each person a turn and help them map as many associations, congregations, and businesses as they can where they know one of the leaders, or know someone who could introduce them to one of the leaders.

Reflection. Use this space to record the main things you want to remember about mapping relationship networks.

Comment: Everyone knows more people than they think they do. After connector-leaders make visible their networks of relationships, they can follow this map into your community where power will grow as connections grow.

Exercise

Buying a Volvo

In a group of three, take fifteen minutes to name all the reasons a person might want to buy a Volvo?

Comment: Use this exercise to practice expanding your sense of the importance of different motivations to act. Imagine that someone wants to buy a new car. There are a thousand different reasons that could motivate this action. A poor salesperson assumes that he knows the customer's reasons. A good salesperson carefully listens to understand the customer's motivation as the best way to make the sale.

Identify an Opportunity for Contribution That Makes Sense

The point of asset mapping is to enroll people, associations, and local institutions as active participants in the community partnerships. Once you have identified them and had learning conversations with their leaders to learn about them, its time to get a "yes", a clear commitment to contribute.

Gaining commitment is a matter of identifying an opportunity for contribution that makes sense from the point of view of the contributor. In thinking about the invitation to contribute, remember the principle: **start with a question, not an answer.** The primary purpose of reaching out is not to assign items from your to-do list to someone else, but to mobilize diverse community assets to address an important issue. This means helping people and associations figure out ways to connect to the community partnership that engage their gifts and promote their self-interest. Ask, "What do they want to do?" and "How could we plug them into our work to do what they want to do?"

If a community partnership interested in promoting literacy has decided that a tutoring program is the answer, its representatives will be thinking "How can I sell them on tutoring" as the background of their conversations. To map and mobilize assets, it is far better to hold up a different question: "What might they really want to offer that will grow literacy in our community?"

Learning conversations shaped by the question of what a person or group wants to offer may lead to convergence with the community partnership's current thinking. "Our group could supply tutors for the program the community partnership wants to set up." But conversations might lead to the creation of something no one has thought of yet. "Our group could sponsor a community celebration that honors people who have learned to read and their tutors." or "Some of our members could fix up recycled computers to give literacy students access to e-mail and the internet." or "We know some people who live on the streets that we think would make great tutors and we'd be prepared to support them to learn how to do that."

What matters in asset mapping is a genuine interest in learning how an issue looks from other's point of view and a desire to offer as many people and groups as possible the best chance to contribute to developing their community's capacity to deal with an important issue.

What if people and associations don't want to participate? If an issue doesn't tap motivation to act, it's not a good issue, no matter how important it may be to those who are trying to mobilize a community to act on it. Those who want community change can learn from business on this point. Business people try very hard not to do anything without a market. It may be that trying to organize on a particular issue violates the principle, **never do anything nobody wants.** If no one in a community sees that it will make them stronger to participate, it's time for another round of learning conversations to gain a deeper sense of what people are motivated to act on.

The primary purpose of reaching out is not to assign items from your to-do list to someone else, but to mobilize diverse community assets to address an important issue

Capacity Is The Point

Beth Mount

However much study may be given to the elimination of crime and wrong-doing from the world, true redemption, the turning of evil into good, will in the future depend upon whether true art is able to pour a spiritual substance into the hearts and souls of men.

–Rudolf Steiner
The Spiritual Being of Art

I learned about The Point, a community center in Hunts Point, the Bronx, New York City, during a visit there in March, 2006. I'm involved with parents of young people with disabilities in New York City who are searching for new work and living options using the ABCD community building approach. I work to create imaginative futures for young people in some of the most labeled neighborhoods in New York City and my visit to The Point affirmed the assumption that the good can be found and nurtured in all people, in the bleakest places, through creative community action.

To understand the inspiring impact of a visit to The Point, one must appreciate the neighborhood context. Hunts Point is historically one of the most beleaguered neighborhoods in New York City. Even today, in 2006, it is known as a breeding ground for gang activity and crime. Hunts point is "off the beaten path" in the Bronx, so its hinterland location invites an "out of sight, out of mind" mentality for community development activists. Mention that you are going to Hunts Point, and those who (think they) know will provide a long list of warnings:

"Don't take the subway."

'Take a gun if you go and don't even think about going there at night."

"That's where the mafia dumps dead bodies."

"That's where the fish are delivered to NYC, and so it stinks. In more ways than one"

"All the old car part dealers in the city are there –don't leave your car long enough to have it taken apart and sold off in pieces."

Broken people, dead bodies, dismembered car parts and dead fish –Hunts Point has served as a repository for the discarded, dark sided, invisible remnants of NYC life. However, there is a small group of people, and one man in particular, Angel Rodriquez, who never took their eyes off the hearts and souls of the people, and so these devoted activists work together to spin the dark into light, to put some of the pieces together again.

Angel grew up in Hunts Point. His mother still lives "over there"; he waves in recognition and says hello to everyone. Angel single handedly promotes the great legends of the Puerto Rican music beat; he sadly recounts his many childhood friends who have been killed or otherwise lost to crime; he enthusiastically lists the artists, musicians, and entrepreneurs who have transformed their lives through creative spirit; and he joyfully invites others to connect to the remarkable refuge of his beloved community center, The Point.

Beth Mount

A visit to The Point, is a visit to a beacon of hope, a sign of collective goodness, a true work of artistic redemptive accomplishment that defies all despairing odds. There is a great spirit in this place, a reflection of those who never lost faith in people and the power of art to bring spirit in.

The Point, the community center, was once a 14,000 square foot bagel factory. Now the space shelters a creative microcosm of the goodness of Hunts Point. A large, open, sky-lit central space is defined by a performance theater on one end, and a dance/karate studio at the other. These bookend spaces are healing places where Angel brings together warring gangs to compete through hip hop, dance, and drumming. Hostile aggression has been transformed into creative expression in these studios, and everything else in the building reflects the many ways that young people are making their artistic mark as an alternative to crime.

The open space is filled with nooks and crannies that provide pathways to creative life. Within the central space tables and chairs serve the café during eating hours, become desks for the children involved in after school tutoring programs, and become a sanctuary for poetry and story telling during evenings and weekends. A photography studio and gallery is nestled between a soul food cafe and an art studio. Art for sale by local youth fills the large open central space, and a staircase ascends to a study hall loft designed for teenagers. Several small local non-profit organizations and small businesses also open off the main hall. Two well-established graphic design studios are operated by successful entrepreneurs who made it in the corporate design world but choose to stay close to home. Tiny, sole proprietor retail businesses incubate here as well.

The Point community center is like a heart that beats, sending creative juices into the far reaching corners of the neighborhood. A neighborhood walk with Angel is a tour of embodied capacity work. Small, renovated, mixed income housing units are sprinkled throughout the community. A new fitness center rises up out of a former prostitution park. A beautiful new waterside park is being carved out of the trash left to rot by the riverside. This corner is where so-and-so's son was gunned down, while that corner and flower garden has been lovingly restored by the owner of the corner store.

Suddenly Angel has to leave to teach a music class at the local public school. It is never too early to find the artistic gifts in these children, and Angel is determined to bring them into the shelter of his community's heart, where they will find their own dance and bring their own beat into the world.

The Point Mission Statement

We work with our neighbors to celebrate the life and art of our community, an area traditionally defined solely in terms of its poverty, crime rate, poor schools, and sub standard housing. We believe the area's residents, their talents and aspirations, are The Point's greatest assets. Our mission is to encourage the arts, local enterprise, responsible ecology, and self-investment in the Hunts Point community.

www.thepoint.org

Inclusion

Person-Centered Work

Community-Centered Work

The move is from
services to clients
to
supports for citizens.

VII
Building the Bridge From Client to Citizen

Inclusion: A Better Way

ABCD organizing mobilizes a community to recognize and act on the conviction that **there is no one we don't need**. The first step is recognizing how many people are at risk of being left out. Many people whose gifts are hidden under labels may be physically present but live at a distance from community life, as clients of human services, living with other clients in group homes, nursing homes, and institutions or in isolation in single rooms or In their family homes.

Others are marginalized by poverty. It is as if a river divides communities, separating citizens from clients.

> **Some of the Labels That Predict Living as a Stranger in the Midst of Community**
>
> Disabled, mentally retarded, mentally ill, welfare recipient, troubled youth, children in foster care, elderly in assisted living and nursing homes, incarcerated mothers, ex-offenders

ABCD organizers encourage and challenge communities to find useful ways to build bridges that invite labeled people to travel from being excluded because of their labels to being included for their gifts, from receiving services as clients to contributing as citizens. This transformation of community life requires change on both sides of the bridge. Citizens need to find practical ways to expand their own circles of relationship, action, and meaning to make room for the contributions of people who may at first seem to have little to offer or who may need some support in order to participate. The move is from exclusive to inclusive community. At the other end of the bridge, the human services that some excluded people count on for assistance need to find ways to provide

> **Our purpose is not so much to help poor people as to build a better community for us all.**
>
> –Lois Smidt
> Beyond Welfare

the help people require in ways that do not deprive them of the responsibilities and rewards of citizenship. The move is **from services to clients to supports for citizens**. Citizens find ways to say to disconnected people, "We need you. You are welcome. Join us." Services find ways to say to disconnected people "We will work with you to figure out how you get the assistance you need to contribute as a citizen."

I once worked for a week in Boise, Idaho. I ate lunch each day in a popular restaurant operated by people with chronic mentally illness. The formula for their success was simple: great food, quick service, and low prices. One day, I sat by myself at a little table near the kitchen. My table was next to a larger table which seated a group of clients of the mental health system. Though the group at the table and the group in the kitchen shared a common label, I heard two very different conversations. From the kitchen I heard the talk of cooks; from the neighboring table I heard the talk of clients. The cooks were talking about making burgers, who was working too slow, who needed to pay more attention –complaining, complimenting, problem solving: the joking and energy of productive people. In contrast to the producer talk of the cooks, the clients' table conversation was consumer talk: which psychiatrist gave the best medications, which drugs had best benefits, how to get off work when you wanted -the talk of people trying to make the mental health system work for themselves. Energy was low and the topic was what service providers could or would not do for them. The ten foot distance from kitchen crew to client group was the distance from heaven to hell. The cooks making and profiting from the burgers; the clients waiting to consume them.

Our challenge and opportunity is to build bridges that will allow more clients to act as citizens, more consumers to become producers.

Seeing With Citizen's Eyes

As a parent of a person with a developmental disability, I am struck by how hard it is for people with disabilities, parents, service providers, and disability advocates to think, look, or act for new possibilities outside the special world of disability services. The maxim, "If you can't see it; you can't do anything with it" describes the problem. The wider community does not see people with developmental disabilities as gifted and the world of people with developmental disabilities does not see the wider community as filled with assets and meaningful opportunities. This shapes people with developmental disabilities and their allies to see the community as an un-welcoming, even dangerous place and to withdraw into special, protected places. This self-restriction feeds the common belief that people with developmental disabilities have nothing to offer and belong in special places. The way out of this trap is to learn to see with citizen's eyes

We are deeply conditioned to think that the service tool is the only tool we have. This locks us into programs, with their tendencies to inflexible, controlling hierarchy and standardized ways of working. It leaves out the innovative, personalized energies of people acting together out of self-interest. ABCD practice…

…directs our attention to the assets and resources available in our communities: the people, associations, organizations, and businesses that surround us.

…suggests actions we can take to mobilize these assets: learning conversations focused on discovering opportunities for people with developmental disabilities to contribute, bringing the assets and connections formed through action in the developmental disability world into community partnerships, taking our place among the community's connector-leaders, contributing actively to work on community issues.

Acting to engage everyday life beyond services, we begin to see with new eyes, the eyes of citizens. As we support each other, find the courage to reach out, and harvest the rewards of joining in actions that make the whole community stronger, we will experience and see ourselves and our communities differently.

Exercise

Mapping Relationships

This relationship map clarifies the work necessary to build connections. Take time to fill in the map below to show some of your important relationships and memberships.

1. In the center, **intimacy** circle put the initials of those closest to you. Your life could not be the same without those you put in this circle.

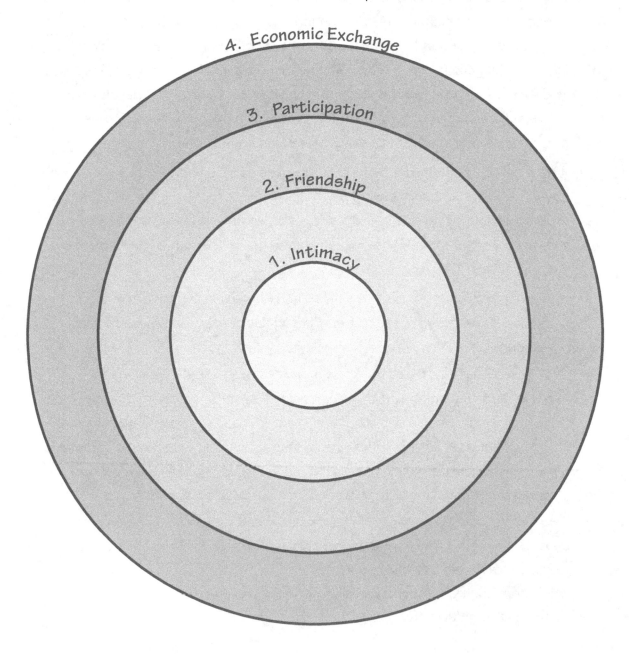

2. In the **friendship** circle, identify those you count on and those who count on you for emotional and practical support and to share good times and hard times.

3. In the third, **participation**, circle identify the associations and groups, formal and informal, to which you belong and in which you contribute as an employee, a member, a leader, or a follower.

4. In the fourth circle, identify relationships that matter to you and **depend on pay** for services or goods. In these significant economic relationships you are client, consumer, or patient.

Comment: The circle of participation is the source of most friendships and intimate relationships other than those that originate in a person's family. Participation and contribution build relationships. Connector-leaders are people with strong investments in the participation circle. In contrast, many labeled people have few entries in the participation circle and so have fewer people in their friendship circle than people with more chances to contribute do. Many labeled people have more people in their circle of economic exchange than people they are connected to through participation: they are more clients and consumers than citizens. A basic goal of ABCD organizing is to expand the contribution circle, both by reaching out to engage more and more people in community development activities and by organizing specific initiatives to connect disconnected people.

Group Discussion In a group of three, discuss what you have learned by mapping your relationships. In your experience, what works to build a person's circle of participation? How do people move from shared participation to friendship?

Reflection. Use the space below to record what you want to remember from the Relationship Map.

Inclusion Takes Both Person-Centered AND Community-Centered Work

ABCD's particular contribution to inclusion comes from its focus on the whole community rather than on individuals. Its goal is to grow the conviction that **there is no one we don't need** and develop meaningful action from this conviction. Through ABCD organizing. well-connected people build networks of connections into community life. The question for connector-leaders is, **how do we get everyday community members to be inclusive because they recognize that reaching out to everyone benefits the whole community?**

The social integration of labeled people matters for three reasons. Exclusion costs the labeled person the opportunity to be a productive community member. This deprives the community of whatever contributions the person might offer. And public resources that could be better used to support people to contribute as citizens are tied up in keeping people on the edge of the community, dependent and un-productive.

Increasingly, foundations, research organizations, and policy makers recognize that there has to be a better way of responding to marginalized people than the current programs-for-clients model. Existing programs may provide specific kinds of necessary assistance, but they generally do not offer a bridge to productive citizenship. In fact, surrounding disconnected people with services that professionally define needs and then try to meet them can weaken people. The rising costs of defining people as needy and trying to comprehensively fill those needs with services can divert investment away from citizen initiatives and toward programs. Intentional relationships, not service programs build bridges from the edge to the center of community life.

A community in which ABCD organizing is active allows human service agencies to expand from person-centered work to person-**and**-community centered work. A growing number of human service organizations are finding person-centered ways to build connections between individual labeled people and citizenship roles. If Phil is an artist with a developmental disability, then the people around him help Phil connect to local opportunities for artists.

To learn more about person-centerd work, see John O'Brien & Beth Mount (2005). *Make a Difference: Person-Centered Direct Support*. Toronto: Inclusion Press. www.inclusion.com

ABCD organizing brings a community-centered dimension to complement this person-centered effort. It asks, How could we organize the whole community to provide many more opportunities for artists, including artists with disabilities? This question leads to many possibilities...

...organize a group of already successful artists to work together to develop more ways that aspiring new artists can develop and offer their gifts

...organize art buyers who appreciate outsider artists to expand the market for the work of artists who have come late to formal training

...shape a new market among congregations, disability rights organizations, neighborhood associations, and local small business associations who would buy art as an expression of their diverse self-interests.

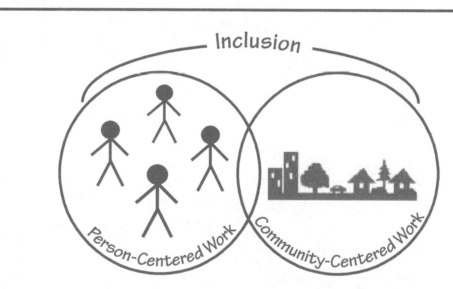

Inclusion

Person-Centered Work

Community-Centered Work

- Support identification of gifts
- Help labeled people to make connections with non-labeled people & associations.
- Provide the personal assistance individuals require in order to participate & contribute

- Act on the conviction "there is no one we do not need" in every community development activity.
- Purposely build networks of connection between labeled & non-labeled citizens
- Organize specifically around increasing the participation of marginalized people in community life.

Exercise

Strangers in Our Midst

In a small group, list all the labels for groups of people who are at the margin, excluded from participation and contribution. Estimate how many people in your community might be in each label category and make a grand total. Then identify the costs of these exclusions to your community. Finally, brainstorm ideas for involving the excluded.

Reflection: Use this space to record the most important things you have learned from this discussion. Be sure to capture ideas for inclusion that you want to put into practice.

Comments: Most people are shocked at how many people are excluded. This simple exercise raises awareness of the costs of community disconnection and, even more important, it lays a foundation for "insiders" to begin to see "outsiders" as a hidden and untapped resource.

Organizing From the Conviction That "There Is Nobody We Don't Need"

Make a habit of two things: help or at least do no harm.
—Hippocrates

Community development efforts help when they reach out and engage people who are excluded because of their label or social status in actively addressing issues that matter to the whole community. Overcoming exclusion begins with including labeled people in the learning conversations that define the issues that matter and proceeds through every step of the community organizing process. Providing people with practical ways to pursue their dreams and give their gifts by joining their fellow citizens in action that is meaningful for all breaks the cycle of exclusion and enriches everybody.

Engaging people who are likely to be left out takes consciousness and discipline, but the necessary attitudes and actions are within anyone's reach, as Jody Kreitzman's *Ten Commandments for Youth Involvement* on the next page shows. Although written about involving youth, these precepts apply to any excluded group. Connecting some excluded people will take some extra effort. Some people don't drive and live in places where public transportation isn't convenient, affordable, and accessible; they will need a ride. Some people need physically accessible places for their wheelchairs. Some people need help eating. Some people don't read and write. Some people's ways of communicating take some getting used to. Most of the accommodations that people need are easily made by following the lead of the person and those who know the person best.

> **You find friends by making the sandwiches at the food pantry not by standing in line to get the sandwiches.**
>
> **—A community leader**

Community development efforts hurt when organizers and leaders fall for the mistaken idea that labeled people lack the capacity and desire to work for a better community for everyone. This reduces potential contributors and friends to no more than clients. It can even lead to community development

Ten Commandments for Involving Young People in Our Communities

Jody Kreitzman

1. Always start with the gifts, talents, knowledge and skills of young people. Find out what they like to do and are good at doing.

2. Always look for the positive in the unique individual. For example, it should be, "Maria with the lovely voice," not, "Maria the pregnant teen."

3. Every community is filled with useful work and service opportunities for young people. The corollary of this is that there is no community, institution or organization that cannot find a useful role for a young person.

4. Always distinguish between real work and games or simulations, because young people can.

5. Fight age segregation. Youth today are the most age-isolated generation in our history, to everyone's detriment.

6. Avoid aggregating people, especially young people, by what they don't have. Too often, we group people by their deficiencies instead of letting those who can help those who can't.

7. Move as quickly as possible beyond "youth advisory boards" or committees with only one youth on them.

8. Constantly cultivate opportunities for young people to teach and lead.

9. Constantly reward and celebrate creativity, energy and effort — loudly and with spirit. Whenever possible, let young people take the lead on the form the celebration will take.

10. Amplify continuously "we need you." Young people are not a problem, they are our solution.

efforts that define and treat people as clients or as less fortunate objects of pity and charity. This turns what is distinctive about Asset Based Community Development upside down: instead of looking for and mobilizing assets, it focuses on deficiencies; instead of expressing the creativity of people, it harnesses people to operate programs; instead of bringing people into contributing citizenship, it creates clients. Whenever it comes up, ABCD organizing confronts the idea that some people have to be "done to" and "done for"

with the truth, everyone has gifts that count. Some people need well organized and publicly funded personal assistance. But the focus of that assistance must be on enabling participation. The benefits that follow from seeing gifts instead of deficiencies bring local leaders to make statements that might sound puzzling to those trapped in seeing only clients: statements like, "Our purpose is not to help people. Our purpose is to build a different kind of neighborhood for us all."

> **A community or person should have to give permission to be helped, particularly to have help increased. The assumption is often that all help is good.**
>
> **– Judith Snow**

To read about seven communities organizing to connect excluded people and what they have learned, see *Hidden Treasures: Building Community Connections by Engaging Gifts* by Susan Rans with Mike Green.* Some of these organizing initiatives, like Boston's **Dudley Street Neighborhood Initiative**, purposely including people likely to be left out is one aspect of the way the organization goes about its work of neighborhood rebirth. In others, like Seattle's **Involving All Neighbors**, mobilizing connections among labeled people is the purpose of the initiative. In all seven communities, local people have…

…built involvement based on appreciation of people's gifts and dreams

…protected citizen space by respecting the distinctive contributions of people and programs

---

*Download from www.mike-green.org

...invested in connectors, people who make it their concern to reach out and bring new people in.

Exercise

Welcoming the Newcomer

Imagine that Mike is a good friend who has just moved to your community and knows no one but you. Spend 20 minutes in a small group generating ideas for helping Mike become a member of your community. What would you ask Mike? What would you do to help him get involved? What opportunities would you expect to develop for Mike once he starts to participate in and contribute to your community?

Reflection: Use this space to record what you have learned. Think about what works to welcome a newcomer. Identify any actions you might take to begin to see the strangers in the midst of your community with citizen's eyes.

Comment: Often people act as if making connections with people and associations were either too complicated to imagine or just a matter of fate, something that either happens or does not. In fact, intentional action can build participation and relationships. What sometimes blocks the action necessary is a failure to see with citizen's eyes and notice the assets a person can offer and the opportunities to mobilize those assets.

When Connection Is the Point

As more communities become aware of the costs of exclusion, more connector leaders identify mobilizing the assets of excluded people as an issue worth addressing in its own right. The focus of these ABCD organizing efforts is on bringing people over the bridge from clienthood into a contributing role in any community association or project that matches their personal interests and allows them to give their gifts. These connecting projects have had such purposes as re-capturing the energies and contributions of elders or connecting people with developmental disabilities to opportunities to be contributing members of community organizations.

Acting On the Principles for Successful Relationship Building

The principles for successful relationship building are clear. They grow from a simple human truth: when people come together out of care and share in meaningful action, important personal connections result.

- Relationships grow from participation and contribution.
- Contribution begins in identifying the gifts a person has to give.
- To discover where to seek opportunities for people to share their gifts, ask, "Where does this person's gift make sense? "
- To make the bridge, find connectors in the place where the person's gifts make sense. Who, on the inside of this association or project, can welcome and introduce and support the beginnings of belonging?
- People who rely on services may need some extra help to adjust the assistance they get from those services in order to make their participation easier.

An example. A person who loves to sing hymns finds a place in her church choir with the thoughtful support of a veteran choir member. Her personal assistants adjust their schedules to take account of her choir practices.

Building good bridges means working from both sides of the river. Excluded people may not see themselves as having gifts that could be valuable to their fellow citizens. They may need coaching to discover their gifts and follow a path to participation. The process outlined on the following pages lets people and their coaches put the principles for successful relationship building into action.

Harmonizing the Four Elements of a Human Support System and Finding the Next Steps

Judith Snow

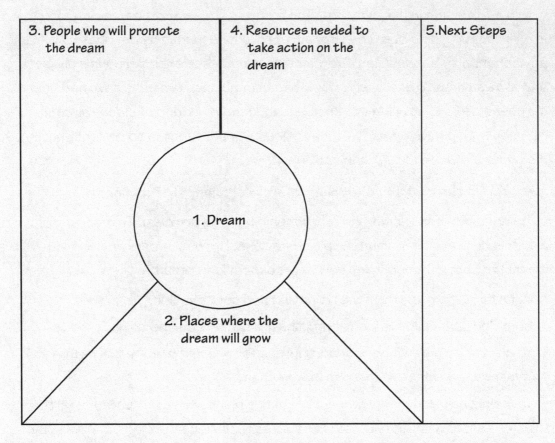

People's dreams provide a key to understanding people's gifts and what's needed to give them. Everyone needs a support system in order to pursue their dreams and give their gifts. The fundamental principle of this process is that the integrity of any human support system depends on the harmony or coherence of four elements. These elements are dream, or vision, places or locations, relationships, and resources. In order to plan for the future, or to resolve a problem or crisis, it is necessary to examine and align the four elements, in the order indicated. As you discover the proper alignment of these elements, action steps become evident.

Stop the process as soon as you identify one to four *Next Steps*. Start again at *Dream* as soon as you complete these steps. This process works best when you use it for frequent, brief review and realignment of the four elements.

Dream. All activity must be based in a vision of what the person is inspired to accomplish. It is not important for this vision to be "realistic". It is important that the person authentically desire the dream or vision.

Places. Everything in life takes place somewhere. Places, especially rooms and buildings that have been constructed with a purpose in mind, reflect and potentate the likelihood of certain dreams being fulfilled there. Other dreams will not be reflected or even will be actively suppressed in the same location. In addition, very similar locations develop different cultures, practices and ambience. Pay careful attention to selecting the places to explore a dream.

People. People behave differently with each other and will offer or withhold informal and formal support to each other in relationship with the place they are in and to the understanding they have of the person's dream. Pay attention to where and how people are introduced to an invitation to get involved. It makes a powerful difference. It is also powerful to invite people to become involved simply because they are in the right place. People in the right place will bring knowledge, insight and resources to a dream that other people have no awareness or facility with.

Resources. The resources that are actually required to move a dream toward fulfillment are often very different from the resources you imagine will be needed when you begin the process. Consequently, it works best to consider this element last. It is typical in our culture to block action by thinking first of resources: "I'd like to go to Italy but I don't have the money" won't get you to Italy. On the other hand, fulfillment requires control over the right resources. When the necessary resources are absent, or the person is denied access to them, the question of how to obtain these necessary resources becomes the *Dream*, and the cycle of alignment is repeated to reveal new *Next Steps* toward necessary resources.

Next Steps and Return to the Dream Taking the *Next Steps* changes the person's understanding and articulation of the *Dream*. Finding and being in different *Places* changes the person's understanding and articulation of the *Dream*. Introducing the *Dream to People* changes the person's understanding and articulation of the *Dream*. Applying *Resources* changes the person's understanding and articulation of the *Dream*. Consequently, no alignment can stay in place very long in any human endeavor. In order to sustain passion and creativity it is essential to revisit the harmonization cycle frequently.

---

*For more on this process and on the relationship of dreams and gifts, see Judith Snow, *What's Worth Doing*. Toronto: Inclusion Press www.inclusion.com.

The heart of bridge building between excluded people and opportunities for participation is in the same place as any other form of ABCD organizing: in learning conversations. Learning conversations with labeled people, like learning conversations with other citizens, focus on the same fundamental questions: what, in our community, do you care about enough to act on, what do you have to offer, and what will it take for you to join in action with others who share your interest? Sometimes it takes extra energy and imagination to discover the ways that someone who has been seen as needy is needed in their community. Sometimes people take in the idea that they have nothing to offer except their need for help and think of themselves in terms of what they receive instead of what they can give. Sometimes people have no or very limited language and count on others to interpret for them. In these situations, the form of learning conversations needs creative adjustment. Two examples:*

- Sometimes holding a learning conversation about people's interests and gifts with a group of people who know and care about a person both reveals the foundation for that person's participation and mobilizes the necessary support for action. There are variety of ways to organize these group learning conversations, called person-centered planning.

- Some people benefit from the support of a group who commit themselves to promoting people's participation. These groups are sometimes called Circles of Support.

How To Start an ABCD Connections Project

The getting started group. The first step is to form an initiating group to prepare for a connections project. This group is best made up of a mix of local leaders with access to needed resources from government, non-profit organizations, and businesses and local citizen leaders with strong relationships who have wisdom about the local community and the connections and trust necessary to mobilize its inhabitants. This group answers these questions about the connections project:

- In what geographical area will the connections project work?

---

*A good place to start learning about these ways of extending learning conversations is John O'Brien and Connie Lyle O'Brien, *A Little Book About Person-Centered Planning*. Toronto: Inclusion Press. www.inclusion.com

- What group of labeled people will the connecting project engage?

- Which local citizens are the best prospects to joining the connector-leader group for the project? An effective connector-leader group will reflect the diversity of the community: neighborhoods, ethnic groups, religious groups, associations, business, and agencies,

- Where will the initiating group secure funding to pay one connector-organizer for at least three years?

- Who will the initiating group hire as the paid connector organizer? (See the description of this role on the next page.)

- What doors need opening before the work of connecting particular people begins? Consider human service agencies, mutual aid groups for labeled people or their families, advocacy groups, media, law enforcement and others.

- How will the connector-organizer get guidance and direction while organizing the connector-leaders group? (Once the connector-leaders group is formed, the initiating group backs off and the connector-leader's group make the connections between labeled people and the community as well as steer the project and guide their organizer.)

- How will the connector-organizer learn and develop more skills and knowledge? Who should the connector-organizer visit to learn about the work? Who will consult with the connector-organizer and the project?

The connector-leaders group: The connector-leaders group will listen to the dreams, interests, and gifts that labeled people want to offer. They will then figure out good places for people to contribute and use their personal connections, trust, and influence to open doors and assure that people are welcomed, and that people have what they need to sustain participation for as long as they choose. The connector-organizer works for the connection group, helping the group make connections and assisting them to keep connections strong. The connector-leaders group will deal with these questions:

- What is our project's name and what identity should it have in our community?

- What is our vision for the connections project and what long-term and annual goals do we have for our project?

The Connector-Organizer

The connector-organizer builds a citizens' organization for inclusion, connects people, and supports those connections.

A good guide has certain characteristics:

- Really knows 'All people have gifts' — no exceptions.
- Knows your community is a good and welcoming place.
- Likes and enjoys people.
- Build relationships very well.
- Persuasive-- Can influence people and can close the deal.
- Determined-- Can hear *no* and continue.
- Thoughtful -- Can keep focus and make plans.
- Seasoned student of human relations: can address the complications that come up when a group of people work together.
- Creative problem solver who can help other people invent answers
- Can work through others and handle ambiguity and uncertainty without going crazy.

The initiating group looks for specific evidence of these attributes in a candidate organizer's actual experience. Aspiration is not enough.

- What is the connection projects' annual plan and budget. What is the 3-5 year plan?

- How will we learn even more effective ways to identify people to connect. This includes learning more effective ways to identify people, mobilize people to recognize and act on what they care about, support and challenge people to see and give their gifts, and negotiate for the adjustments that people need in order to sustain satisfying participation.

- How will we learn even more effective ways to discover connection possibilities among local residents, associations, congregations, business, non-profits, and government agencies?

From services to services and connecting.

Human service agencies offer useful assistance to disconnected people, but services alone cannot lead a person into community. People enter community through active participation and contribution in the activities that weave the tapestry of community life. The challenge for ABCD connections organizing is to build bridges from the edge of the community, where people are clients, to the center of the community, where people are needed citizens. Denver's mayor recently said it costs his city $40,000 a year in public funds to maintain one homeless person. What if that $40,000 per homeless person were less focused on maintaining people in shelters and emergency services and more focused on their social and economic integration?

The ABCD organizing framework shows a way to building these bridges. It guides people to see answers to these critical questions.

Assets. What are the hidden gifts among the strangers in the midst of community? Where are the places for connection and the resources to support connections?

Organizing. How can groups of well-connected people work together to use their relationships to include an ever-wider circle of their community?

Leading by stepping back: how can helping agencies move from only offering services to investing substantially in both services **and** local ABCD connections work.

ABCD and Inclusion.

Janice Fitzgerald

When we enter the disability world, parents lose the perspective taken for granted when raising typically developing children. When parents and providers of services can't get beyond the "disability world", they decide, consciously or unconsciously, to divide the world into places where people with disabilities can belong and places where they don't belong. Plain and simple, we participate in exclusion while we talk about inclusion.

As director of Parent to Parent of New York State, I am frequently at the table for discussions about serving and supporting people with disabilities in inclusive environments. Oftentimes, these groups involve only people from state and local disability agencies talking to each other.

This talk is sometimes about adults who lead isolated lives and their need for individualized services. There is no doubt that a change to individualized services is crucial in a service system focused on generating "billable units" by providing clinical services and skill building that is disconnected from ordinary life. But services, no matter how good, can never substitute for community life; so individualized services can't be the panacea for social exclusion. Around these tables, where people in the disability world worry about isolation, there is little talk of substantial investment in activities that build relationships. This is partly because agencies and government entities do not know how to facilitate relationships, and partly because their managers do not believe that relationships truly matter.

Parents recognize that individualized services are important, but they also recognize that services can break down, leaving the person ultimately reliant on their parents and any other people who have a committed relationship with them. Parents have learned that when each family works alone, they will always be alone. It is only other people that can keep our kids safe. This understanding has given rise to organizations like Parent to Parent. Many of these parent driven organizations have recognized that government disability programs and disability service providers can't break through to supporting people in a web of good community relationships without a lot of help.

How do we move from services to community life? First, step back and remember what a real life in community looks and sounds like.

Community looks like children playing on a playground; it looks like friends sharing the joys of having children. It sounds like a day at the ocean with lots of pails

Janice Fitzgerald

and shovels and kids laughing and crying. Community looks like going to concerts, theatre, skiing, art classes, and plain having fun! Real lives balance work and play.

Real life looks like my two older sons starting out on their own, doing their grocery shopping, laundry, sharing an apartment, not having enough money to cover rent because they spent it going out every night, and scrambling to get odd jobs to cover their screw up. It sounds like a group of friends just hanging out and talking.

Real life is having a circle of participation, where we are by choice and because of what we are interested in. It is in this circle of connections and associations that we have opportunities to give our gifts. This is where we cultivate relationships and friendships and where inner circles are built.

Families must believe that their child belongs in everyday life. If they do not model that, then no one else will. Every child should have the opportunity and right to participate in everyday activities, and to have the individualized supports to make that happen.

It's essential to create and keep a non-threatening, safe space to help a person dream and believe. When people have a vision —a graphic image that captures their dream and shows a path toward it— they feel the courage to reach out for the connections that build community.

Successful community inclusion happens when people get to know someone as a person, not as a client. Inclusion cannot work or be successful just because there is a law in place. Only other people can make the world an inclusive place.

p2pnys@adelphia.net

www.parenttoparentnys.org

The Evolution of Helping

Terry Pickett

Just what exactly is this thing – BW (Beyond Welfare)? I think I would answer differently at different times in my life in this community, but for right now BW is a "locus of community." It is a place, a time, a date in which a community comes together face-to-face. The community does its work throughout the week, but every Thursday at 5:30-8:00 PM the community happens in front of its members. The essence of that community is building relationships across race and class lines. If we do nothing else, we meet on level ground every week. These are authentic relationships characterized by intimacy and reciprocity. And that is a heuristic and powerful platform. It produces learning and transformation for all members of the community, albeit in a gradual and sneaky way. You don't know it's happening, at first; in retrospect it just seems to have happened. But, when you are conscious of the changes, you try to be disciplined about the behaviors that enable these level relationships to continue and deepen. I will return to this idea shortly, but some digressions will help readers better understand what I experience and feel in the BW community.

A lot of what has happened to me in BW can be traced through the stages of helping, at least as I have experienced them. **Stage 1: Helping as Fixing.** I got involved in BW in a search for ways to give back to my community. I had done well in this community, and I realized that my doing well was not entirely due to my own talents: being white, male and educated had a lot to do with it. Likewise I realized that **not** doing well could not be solely attributed to one's lack of talents or industry. So I was looking for a way to "help those less fortunate" than myself. These were great motives, but also grounded in some implicit models of which I thought I was aware. My helping was to fix what was wrong. After all, I was talented, disciplined, and successful. I knew a thing or two about encountering and surmounting problems. So off to fixing I went… softly. I really didn't want to fix people, but that is how I approached it. I knew some things that others could use; then they, too, would be successful. My underlying model was that there was something missing in others. My job was to fill that in. Martin Buber would call this an I-It relationship. Well this had its limits; some material success, but the relationships were not satisfying. I felt burdened. And why not, for I had accepted responsibility for someone else's success. In addition, the fixee seemed to have a mind of his/her own. This made my "job" frustrating, as well as difficult. **Stage 2: Helping as Coaching.** Next came working with the other person as a guide, a mentor—to educate and counsel. The difference here is that the other has a perfect right to define what they want

Terry Pickett

and need, and I had a job to instruct about how to fulfill those needs. My role was to assist. This was more comfortable, but still not totally successful nor satisfying to me. There was something missing. I sensed that I was still in a service relationship with the families and individuals with whom I was working. **Stage 3: Helping as Throwing In Together.** This approach has the flavor of "My neighbor needs assistance. Let me ask how I can help." In other words, it is my neighbor who defines their preferred outcome, they define what success looks like, and I offer what I can to them. Buber would call this an I-Thou relationship. I really like this "place." Here I can be helped as well as help; I can share my frustrations and well as listen to the frustrations of others. When the person I have "thrown in with" asks me "How are you doing?" I actually tell them –warts and all. They listen and in doing so I am unburdened and connected.

I have changed as a result of being in this community. I have a wider circle of diverse friends; I am a more informed and compassionate member of civic discussions and decisions; I am getting graceful about following the lead of others; I know myself and where I came from so much more deeply. I often describe this as "Having lived my life as a Jesuit, now I am a Franciscan." What I have learned about myself is significant. I have learned about my class background and have returned to valuing it. My Dad was a powerhouse mechanic, a blue collar worker, and our family was working poor. My parents instilled in all six of their children the value of education. So off we went to college and got graduate degrees and many of us ended up in education. My education (Jesuit for 8 years) "bought" me into the middle class where smarts and degrees and good manners are valued. In the BW community I rediscovered my manual skills – carpentry, plumbing, electrical. I now take great joy in rehabbing, de-junking, reclaiming old computers, and generally being a Mr. Fix-It. I have rediscovered the ways of the working class and I love it. It is also a way for me to honor the honest labor of my parents, my father in particular. There is a life line there that was dormant for many years. This is the Franciscan part of

The greatest poverty we may all face is the poverty of relationship and meaning, not simply too little money.

me: simple, earthy, and plain-spoken. I have not given up the Jesuit skills (as you will see), but now they partner together. I even risk offending the class structure which I sustain and from which I benefit by plainly saying what I see (much as my father did when he would review his citizen work in Model Cities in the 60s at the dinner table).

Even as I like resetting a toilet without a leak, I also spend some good Augustine time making some sense of all of this. I have developed a model for helping me place my experience. Even though the model lists the areas of transformation by size (personal to system), the developmental sequence is different. The transformation begins at the Community level. The immersion there leads to Personal and System explorations (I believe system transformation depends upon personal transformation). And that is one of the jewels of Beyond Welfare. **By fostering a safe place to bridge class and race, an authentic, diverse community unfolds.** The stranger is not strange, simply a neighbor —another member of the community. "Edges" almost cease as our boundaries are so permeable that we have to guard our naiveté at times. In this unfolding one comes to a realization of self —from whence I sprang, how it is I have learned to navigate this world, and what transcendental choices lay before me about how I can navigate in the future. And these wonders spill over into civic life, work life, and home life.

My personal transformation is still in progress. I have been de-acquiring many things: tools, electronics, habits of not offending decision-makers, etc. At the same time I have acquired new ways of seeing the world. These include: insuring that voices of people are included in the design and provision of services, seeing idle resources as wasteful (whether things or people), and realizing that the greatest poverty we may all face is the poverty of relationship and meaning, not simply money. Enough money seduces me into isolation —after all, I can "buy" my way out of most problems until one day I notice that all of my relationships are purchased. In this very real sense the BW community **is** eliminating poverty.

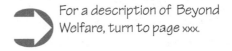 For a description of Beyond Welfare, turn to page xxx.

Personal Transformation

- Living simply
- Sharing resources
- Avoiding hedonistic consumerism
- Countering the politics of greed

A personal commitment to solidarity with those marginalized by poverty

Solidarity entails embracing two realities. 1. It is possible to live rich, rewarding lives & not be wealthy. 2) The worldview & values of the earning class have inherent worth. In fact, it may be the poor who are uniquely situated to guide us in a world of diminishing resources.

Community Transformation

- Mutual and reciprocal relationships across class lines
- Circles of support, family partners & allies
- Mutual respect –dignity of the working class
- Everyone has the resources, relationships, & meaning to thrive

A collective commitment to ending poverty

The core work of BW: crafting an exemplar community within the larger community. This community is attractive to others because it responds to their need for money, meaning, and friends. We are attractive because we practice our core beliefs & values.

System Transformation

- Affordable housing –ownership
- Sustainable wage **jobs** with benefits
- **Childcare:** safe, available, & affordable
- **Transportation:** reliable & affordable – public & private
- **Education** that enables all to succeed without stigma or marginalization
- **Healthcare:** preventive & catastrophic

A just & respectful system

Initiatives to enable systemic change in the conditions that sustain material & spiritual poverty in our community.

Communities Changing the Course of Their Own Development

Gord Cunningham

In 1939, Moses Coady, the man after whom the Institute where Alison Mathie and I work would later be named, published a book called *Masters of Their Own Destiny*. In it he describes how communities scattered throughout northeast Nova Scotia were rebuilding the foundations of their local economies through, producer, consumer and financial cooperatives – a phenomenon that became known as the 'Antigonish Movement'. For Moses Coady the future of these so-called poor and marginalized communities was bright, because as he put it *They will use what they have to secure what they have not*. Moses Coady didn't call what he was doing 70 years ago ABCD, but he was describing it; citizen-led development that combined natural resources with people's skills, capacities, savings and social capital to re-build communities and local economies.

Everywhere in the world Alison and I travel today we ask people to tell us stories about a time when people from that village or neighborhood mobilized their own assets and successfully undertook an initiative without any direction from outside individuals or agencies. Even in the poorest or most remote communities we always find lots of great stories. If you peel back a layer on these stories you will always find examples of local leadership that focused on opportunities rather than problems, and informal associations of people motivated by a sense of civic duty, at the center of the action. There is much that government and non-governmental organizations can learn from these experiences about how to "lead by stepping back".

For example, just ten kilometers down the Trans Canada Highway from the Coady International Institute there is a rural farming community of 1,100 households called St. Andrews. Over the last 17 years people in this community have managed to build a community centre, a curling rink and seniors housing apartments, and they have done this almost entirely with their own savings, skills, labour and materials. Community members have been very clear that the community centre and curling rink could and should be built without any government assistance. The seniors housing apartments on the other hand needed a 25% government investment to bring down the rents to a point where the units would be affordable for local seniors. To most rural communities in Nova Scotia today a local development project consists mainly of writing a funding proposal to government. St. Andrews serves as an excellent example of how communities can take a lead in rebalancing the rights and responsibilities of citizens, communities and the State.

Gord Cunningham

Unfortunately we have also found that when we ask development practitioners (and we've asked hundreds who have attended the Coady Institute over the past 8 years) to tell us stories about citizen-led initiatives from their own experiences, very few of them can find even one example that is in any way related to their work. Instead, they usually have to think of the village where they grew up, or the neighborhood where they are currently living to find such a story. Not surprisingly, their involvement in these stories is never as a "development practitioner" - it is always as a contributing member or citizen.

What I have learned from these kinds of stories continues to reinforce what John McKnight, Jody Kretzmann and Mike Green have been saying for years. Development is really all about stimulating that virtuous spiral of assets and agency (the capacity to act) that is created when people begin to reclaim the space for citizens to lead. I can think of no better example of this than the story of my own mother and favorite aunt. From the late 1950s to the mid 1970s these two women were preoccupied with raising their families. When their youngest children reached high school they decided they would start a restaurant. In order to make this dream a reality they drew on a variety of modest assets: a shared passion for good food; the skills and experience in cooking for others they had acquired over the years; the equity they had both accumulated in their homes; a wealthy brother-in-law; and the talents of their respective husbands in carpentry and bookkeeping. Over the next ten years as they built the business they acquired new equipment, skills, relationships, and income. They also began to be seen by others (and to see themselves) differently. In addition to being mothers and wives they became employers, managers, large-scale purchasers, members of business and trade associations and neighborhood philanthropists. Whether we are talking about a group of women in rural Ethiopia or a group of volunteer firemen in St. Andrews or my mother and aunt, the process seems to be the same.

> **They will use what they have to secure what they have not.**
> – Moses Coady

Alison and I have come to believe that it is critically important for development practitioners to occasionally look away from their institutions' projects and programs to find out what communities (or even small groups of people) have done, or are doing, without their help. They need to learn from what statisticians would call (and we hate this term but love the concept) "positive deviance". This is done as a matter of course in other fields. For example, medical researchers don't just study sick people, they also try to find out why some people, exposed to the same conditions as those that are ill, remain healthy. But in the development field we tend to only to study those communities where we have been working, or our own "best practices," or those projects that seem to have the best potential for scaling-up.

Alison Mathie

Years ago, when my husband and I spent nine months living in a village in Papua New Guinea, I was forced to face my failings —neither able to carry water on my head, nor weave a string bag, nor understand the complexities of subsistence gardening systems, nor fully appreciate the roles and obligations of different members of intricate extended families. Not much was expected of me as an outsider, I was clearly just learning, and people tagged along with me with a mixture of bemusement and patience. But once I

Alison Mathie

came to terms with how little I really understood, it made me think twice before giving advice, whether it was about dealing with headaches (blood letting not a good idea), recommending weaning foods (sago not too nourishing), or helping women to organize across extended family groupings for income generating activities. In other words, the more I got to know people, the less sure I was of my ground. When should I intervene?

Before and since that time I have been involved with government and non-government development workers at the community level, and in the last 10 years with people in management positions supporting extension workers. I am struck by the difficult position in which extension workers or community development workers often find themselves.

Their role typically requires them to deliver services and advice —to identify and solve problems. They feel the burden of expectation that they should be experts. Often they are responsible for measurable outcomes and deliverables. In fact, because they are at the end of the line in a delivery system (whether of information, training, or other services) they assume the role of supplier. They often don't have the luxury of quality time spent with the community, asking questions. In particular, asking questions that assume that community members have strengths, skills, and talents to offer. And in many cases the delivery system is not interested in that knowledge.

In the course of the work Gord Cunningham and I have been doing at the Coady Institute with NGOs trying out ABCD, one of the most dramatic effects is the change in the relationship that the community development worker forges with the community, and the leap in job satisfaction he or she experiences as a result. The first transformation is a new-found respect for people: "I never realized that this community had done so much!" said one fieldworker enthusiastically. He had been working with people in this community for some time, but only now was he asking questions that helped him discover their past achievements. Related to this is the way the fieldworker perceives his or her role. No longer "delivering" development, there is a stronger sense of "co-production". As one fieldworker in the Philippines noted: *Before, people were always waiting for development. So people would wait for me. With ABCD I started to feel less of a burden. I gave my leadership role to others.* Stepping back like that enables the fieldworker to reassess his or her own value, how to best contribute given what the community has the capacity to do for itself, and how to help without undermining that capacity.

Community development workers are usually not independent actors. They work for institutions (whether government, non government or private sector) and these organizations have to provide the support and encouragement for people working at the community level to "lead by stepping back" without renouncing their responsibility to help people bring about the change they want. It means asking very different questions, starting with my own: **Not** When should I intervene? **but...**

...How can I reverse the delivery system so that it is more *inside-out?*

...How can I help people see the possibilities for working together in new ways – men with women, relatively wealthy with the relatively poor, so that they can take action as citizens?

Intervening then becomes something we do as citizens ourselves, building our own communities, and using our own networks and influence to bring about the change that allows other communities to build themselves.

Coady International Institute

www.coady.stfx.ca

Grantmaking to support active citizens

Janis Foster

What can I say about a thirty-year journey that began by accident but so profoundly shaped who I am? Thirty years ago my neighbor Stephanie knocked on my door and invited me to come to a city council meeting. Thirty years ago, I met Agnes Bowe, a tiny, frail from the outside/fearless from the inside woman who fought highways and whatever else threatened her idea of how things should be or how things should happen. And, thirty years ago I met Kay, Sue, Irma, Carl and Julia – neighbors who brought special gifts and wonderful warm hearts to the work of making our throw-away neighborhood a welcoming, fun place to live.

The accident was that thirty years ago I moved into the neighborhood that connected me to these people and others who launched me on a journey that has provided – and is still providing - powerful lessons about people and communities. And when I say people, I include ME. Perhaps the most powerful discoveries along the way have been discoveries about me - my gifts, my passions, my limitations. Moving into this neighborhood – a neighborhood that was challenged by twenty years of red-lining that was the by-product of an interstate highway project – provided the opportunity for me to move from spectator to active citizen.

Because this neighborhood had been so challenged for so long, there was no room on the sidelines. Here I was – new blood added to a well running dry from years of activism. Forget protocol or chain of command. Ms. Bowe was the first to put me to work. And while I was working (running errands, doing research, typing letters, making calls) she was teaching and inspiring. What a difference one person could make. What a bigger difference people together could make. How these little differences added up to big differences. What it means to be an active citizen in a democracy. How it feels to be living in a community where people know each other. What surprising gifts the odd-balls brought to the table. All of these were lessons that changed me in profound ways.

My journey from my neighborhood took me to the Center for Neighborhoods – a weird and wonderful organization that was devoted to helping people like me in organizations like the one in

> **Resisting the lure of the couch and remote control, people were connecting with their neighbors to have fun, offer support, explore common interests, and take care of their community**

Janis Foster

my neighborhood learn the ropes of active citizenship. This stop on my journey brought some surprises, pleasant and not-so-pleasant. I was astounded and energized by the number of people who had *active citizen* in their heart. Against all odds and resisting the lure of the couch and remote control, people were connecting with their neighbors to have fun, offer support, explore common interests, and take care of their community. In my years at the Center for Neighborhoods, I met people who inspired me and kept me going – who I added to my list of personal heroes and role models.

I was also surprised at how differently I was regarded by everyone, from my neighbors to the city's mayor, when I took a position for pay. For some of my neighbors, a salary meant that I had crossed over from *the land of us to the land of them* and lost legitimacy. To the mayor and others in positions of power, I had crossed over from *the land of them to the land of us* and had new legitimacy. People now believed that they understood why I was doing what I was doing: that my primary motivation was to advance my career and make some money. I needed the job and the money, but my real motivation was the taste for active citizenship that I had acquired in my neighborhood.

For the past eighteen years, I have worked for and with funding organizations – community foundations, private foundations, family foundations, United Ways, local governments, and organizational hybrids- that are using money as a lever for community change. I began my work with the Community Foundation of Greater Memphis to launch a new grant program that came to Memphis through a special program of the Charles Stewart Mott Foundation. *The Community Foundations and Neighborhoods Small Grants Program* was the Mott Foundation's invitation to 23 community foundations to get closer to the ground by supporting emerging neighborhood groups in low-income areas of the cities where they worked. I began my job there with knowledge of and comfort with neighborhood groups; what I had to learn was the culture of the funding world - what it meant to be a funder and how I could be effective as the connector between the funding world and the neighborhood world.

Like work in my neighborhood, I found peers in other funding organizations who served as invaluable teachers, counselors, coaches, cheer-leaders, sounding boards. Over a surprisingly short period of time, gatherings and conversations that Rainbow Research facilitated between the community foundations that participated in the Mott Foundation's program created a peer learning network that has endured past the days of the Mott Foundation's program and has evolved over the past fifteen years to Grassroots Grantmakers, the organization I am privileged to serve today as Executive Director.

Grassroots Grantmakers is a network of funders in the United States and Canada who are engaged in very local work in their communities that includes regular people – people in neighborhoods like me, Ms. Bowe, Sue, Carl, Irma, and Julia – as an essential part of their big picture thinking on how to make the community better, stronger, more resilient and more vibrant, today and in the future. What is unique about the funders that we seek out as Grassroots Grantmakers is how they see people like me and my neighbors. While other funders, particularly those who stay safely in the domain of funding established non-profit organizations, engage people as professional service providers or as non-professionals who volunteer to expand the reach and capacity of nonprofit service providers, funders in our network are striving to support people in their active citizen role. I appreciate this so deeply because of my experience in my own neighborhood – feeling in my bones just how different that experience was from the experiences that I had working as a volunteer in the Newborn Center in the hospital or as a volunteer sorting clothes for the clothes closet at my church. And I know that what I was doing as a volunteer was important – but that when I'm in my role of active citizen, I'm in a world of possibilities that is just waiting for me and those around me to spot those possibilities and get rolling.

Writing this reflection has helped me see how many of the lessons from my journey that I have brought to my work with Grassroots Grantmakers. I clearly see the different worlds that unwittingly create some "us and them" thinking that gets in the way of making change. I remember the distrust we felt in our neighborhood for outsiders who came to us with good ideas, and remember the discomfort that people in city government felt when they had to take those good ideas out to the community. I remember how different it was for our community foundation to fund unknown groups and feel as comfortable writing those checks as we were with writing the checks to established non-profits. I remember how surprised our board mem-

> **When I'm in my role of active citizen, I'm in a world of possibilities that is just waiting for me and those around me to spot those possibilities and get rolling.**

bers were on those early site visits to learn about the commitment and enterprising spirit of people in poor neighborhoods who were at work as active citizens. I remember the powerful vibe in the air at our annual Salute to Neighborhoods banquet when many of these different worlds came together for an evening of celebration.

I've begun to see my work at Grassroots Grantmakers as celebrating those people who are internal change agents in their funding organizations, creating more space and comfort with funding from an active citizen point of view – and helping others imagine what else they could do if they are a bit disappointed in impacts they are seeing from work that relies on professional problems solvers and people as volunteers. I often feel like the Wizard of Oz – the tiny man behind the curtain creating some thunder and lightning with the turn of a crank. Topical conference calls, presentations, site visits, peer gatherings, information and referral work, building a website, putting ideas out there via my blog – all of this is designed to help bring more support and more legitimacy to the work of active citizens. Our vision for Grassroots Grantmakers is for funding that "begins with residents" to be in the philanthropic mainstream – for funders to add active citizens to the list of essential elements needed for a strong community and to know what to do and what it takes to nurture and support active citizenship in their community. And for me, this all began by the wonderful accident of landing in a neighborhood where active citizenship was in the air, and people like Agnes Bowe became my teachers.

Grassroots Grantmakers

www.grassrootsgrantmakers.org/

Subscribe to Janis's blog, **Big Thinking on Small Grants**, at
http://feeds.feedburner.com/Janisfostercom

The Community Builder's Pledge

I believe, deep down in my heart, that everyone in our community is gifted - and that in spite of our flaws, failings, and disappointments, there is a world of possibilities in our gifts. I believe that sharing our gifts - our wisdom, know-how, talent, knowledge, passion, and care - is how we become more connected to each other and our community and how we create the type of community that nurtures us. I pledge to look at our community and all of the people who live here - including the strangers among us - with new eyes that help me see the richness within our community and everyday opportunities to connect people to each other and our community through their gifts.

–Janis Foster

Key Ideas in ABCD Organizing

To strengthen community, ● take more responsibility for problem solving & ▲ become investors & supporters: a treasure chest for ●

Successful efforts start inside out. People are more motivated to act when organizing starts with a question of what to do about a community issue that they care about. Far fewer will respond to efforts to recruit participation in someone else's answer.

People are motivated to act on: what they don't want to happen (concerns), what they want to create (dreams), & what they want to contribute (gifts).

Both tools are necessary. In our consumer society, ▲ dominate. This discourages people & overloads programs.

Motivation to act (what will I go out the door & do) is different from opinion (what somebody should do).

2 tools for community problem solving: ▲ programs (focus, uniformity, efficiency) & ● people in associations (creativity, innovation, bringing people together)

Leaders willing to work in the gap between citizens– ▲ have a key role to play.

Connections arise through learning conversations: purposeful efforts to make visible what people care about enough to act.

Community partnerships grow when people discover common ground at the level of their motivation to act

Agencies lead by stepping back

ABCD organizing is the process of bringing people into new relationships to create shared meaning by taking action together to create a desirable future.

A group of connector-leaders, people who have trust & influence among a circle of people they can call on to act, is central to organizing a community partnership

Everyone has a gift; everyone's gift is needed & welcome.

Labels ("disabled", "homeless", mentally ill" etc. can cover up gifts & keep people from contributing.

It takes thoughtful effort to build bridges that people can cross from client to citizen.

A connector-leader group is formed as learning conversations & meetings reveal & connect leader's motivation to act.

Step 1: discover each person's capacities & gifts. Step 2: build connection networks that offer practical ways for each person to join other citizens & give their gifts.

An organizer coaches connector-leaders on how to discover & mobilize community assets,. They do not decide what to do.

Organizations that serve marginalized people need to change so that they support people as citizens & invest in activating community. They become both person-centered & community-centered.

VIII

My Path as an ABCD Organizer

As I finish writing this book, I am very aware of my life passing like watching a leaf floating on a stream. It seems like an hour ago that I was 20. Now I am 59 years old. I have a wonderful wife Carol and daughter Annie (who is 25 years old). My aging has clarified the importance of doing what matters most. I have much energy and enthusiasm for life, yet I truly recognize for the first time now that each moment counts and that life will end. I no longer can fool myself about "if I die" as I now am clear that "I will die". So each day I am grateful for my life and for a meaningful vocation.

I have had three very different professions; business, social work, and community organizing. Each contributed much to who I am today.

Lessons From Life in Business

In my twenties I worked in business and started three companies. One went broke and one is still operating successfully today. What did I learn? You don't ever want to do anything without a market. The question is always, "Does anyone want this enough to buy it?" Another valuable lesson came from my time as a salesman of repairs to oil field heavy equipment. I am not very mechanical and I never understood how to repair the equipment, but I sold a lot of repairs. I had very capable people doing the repair work, but so did the competition. I sold a lot of repairs because I made relationships with people. Business showed me how much relationships matter and that to succeed you need ready customers not potential converts.

Lessons From Life in Social Work

In my thirties I worked as a social worker and family therapist. I saw the negative effects of the diagnostic labels we used. I also saw young people move deeper and deeper into being clients of the service system as they became more and more dependent and disconnected. Once I led a therapy group for violent teenage boys in a locked psychiatric facility. I struggled for several weeks with little progress. It finally dawned on me that I was the only person in the room who knew anything about non-violent behavior, a hopeless situation for change. The group was almost perfectly formed to assure no one could learn about non-violence. Aggregating people on the basis of "what they don't have" is not very helpful and often is destructive.

I also learned that all people have capacity and the resources to address problems. People can do more of what works. People can learn from what works. People know more than they think they know. There is always an exception to any problem situation, a time when the problem is not a problem. This time when the problem is not a problem points to solution.

Otto, who was a wonderful teacher, said to me, "No matter how hard you try to do the wrong thing, it won't make it the right thing." If it doesn't work, then stop. If it works, do more of it. Otto had been only to the sixth grade but had much wisdom hard earned through life. I was much more educated than Otto, yet not very wise at that time in my life. Once Otto said to me," Mike, your problem is you are educated beyond your intelligence." I was furious at his comment but soon realized that he was right. I had trusted experts filled with information more than I trusted my common sense and the wisdom of the people I knew. We live in a world where we are constantly barraged with the message that we don't know what is best. We really do know what to do–if only we can listen to our common sense.

> **The purpose of ABCD is to help people remember what they already know.**
>
> –John McKnight

Lessons From Community Organizing

For more than twenty years I have worked in community organizing and community development. My goal in starting organizing work was to help people without power build power for social change. I realized so clearly from my human service years that people are often trapped in problems they cannot solve alone. Community organizing says, **power is in relationships**. I learned much about the bravery of people acting together to change bad situations. I also saw that people who do not think of themselves as leaders can become confident and effective leaders through organizing.

Many years ago I worked in Commerce City, near Denver, as a social worker in protective services. I looked for neglectful families. I thought of Commerce City as broken and full of deficient needy people. Two years later I started working as an organizer in Commerce City. I was asked to develop a strong leadership group to work on serious toxic waste issues. Privately I thought to myself, "Oh no, I can't possibly find leadership here. I will surely fail." But this time I was looking for strength and competence, not looking for abusive families. I found leaders with great heart and talent who won a very large campaign addressing toxic water problems. The very place which two years before seemed so empty was now so full. I learned that you find what you are looking for. We all create the world we believe in. If you expect brokenness, it is very unlikely you will find gifts and talents. In organizing I learned to take people seriously as competent citizens who also have human difficulties. A person can be depressed and be a responsible leader who delivers. I also learned that intentional relationship building is the most fundamental factor in successful community development.

Lessons From ABCD

When I found ABCD I found a fundamental way to think about my community organizing work. Much community organizing in America has sought to build citizens' power to hold local institutions accountable to solve local problems. But more and more social problems have no institution capable of providing real solutions without help. What is needed are new social inventions that can only come from new partnerships. For example, those organizing to develop strong schools must seek to find and mobilize a wide array of assets working together, rather than demanding that schools deliver solutions without partners.

ABCD organizing brings people into relationship so that they can take collective action on a wide variety of purposes. Community organizations can do economic development, community development, inclusion and social network building, social change, mutual aid, and can be engines of social invention. ABCD also helped me recognize that institutions of business, government, and non-profit agencies all have a critical role to play in developing and strengthening citizen power.

Most importantly, John McKnight helped me see the ABCD **vision of community as a place where everyone is needed**. Community is a place of welcome, hospitality, and friendship. Our great possibility comes from each other. The gift of my community work is to get to experience this fact almost daily. The world is filled with a huge diversity of people and creatures that all together —and only all together— make our world worth living. I think the deepest dream of ABCD is that more and more people can come to see truly there is no one we don't need and that a community without a place for everyone is really a community with a secure place for no one. Finally we are called to be friends.

Writing this book has offered me a chance to reflect on what Henry and I do that is valuable. I have come to appreciate more deeply how important critical thinking is to good work. Why do I do what I do? What works? What doesn't work? What have I learned? When a group of people commit to learn together it is very precious.

John O'Brien and Jack Pearpoint of Inclusion Press have been our editors, publishers, and learning partners for this book and DVD. They have accompanied Henry and me along this path of discovery with patient guidance, and valuable critique. Henry and I do not think we are writers. We very likely would never have written this book or made the DVD without Jack and John. After seeing us work, they asked us and encouraged and challenged us to write this book. They recognized what we could not see so clearly, that this book and DVD was needed.

> **To discover your destiny requires that you have a destiny community that recognizes your gift.**
>
> **– Rudolf Steiner**

This reminds me of the importance of invitation, of asking people to join you, and the importance of saying "yes" when others ask from a place of deep meaning. Community is built through the willingness to act. When Judith Snow, who is a person with a long list of physical disabilities, a very wise philosopher about community and inclusion, and also Annie's Godmother, is asked what builds community she always says, "Asking, more asking, and never stop asking!"

Lessons From Annie

Finally, my journey comes around to my daughter Annie. I know Annie to be a person of great heart, goodness, and laughter, with a lovely singing voice and talent at being a human being. Annie lights up any room where she is present. As her Godmother Judith Snow says, "Annie is here on earth to make people happy. That is her job." Annie expects the best of people, and people usually live up to Annie's expectations in her presence. Annie is an artist at living life fully. Annie is also a person with an intellectual disability who has been labeled "mentally retarded".

For many years I separated my life as community organizer and my life as Annie's father. I honestly could not feel peace with her disability and did not want my place in the world of disability. My work was a separate compartment of my life. I had taken inside me shame about Annie being labeled disabled. This feeling is not about Annie being deficient but about me and how I have been affected by the disability label. I now realize that separating my personal life from my work life has been a way to avoid consciously coming to terms with disability. Writing this book gave me the motivation to reflect on my work and my life and these reflections have lead me to find an integration of my personal and vocational life.

I now realize that being Annie's parent guides my ABCD organizing work in the same way that our experience together fundamentally shapes my personal life. I met John McKnight because of Annie. I came to ABCD because of Annie, and there I met Henry and Jody Kreitzman. I met Jack, John, and Judith at Inclusion conferences in Canada. And now my work has become clearly focused on the question of social integration of marginalized people. I want to discover more and more answers to **this great question: how can communities practically act to welcome and include people on the edge of the community?**

I have found a unity between these two parts of myself. I really know now that being Annie's father is a gift to me, sometimes painful and sometimes wonderous, but essential to what I can offer as a community builder and human being. Judith Snow says, "Every great gift has great suffering, and every great suffering has great gifts." Once many years ago, Judith and I were in a van full of people sliding through Toronto snow late at night after a party, with laughter filling the van. Judith said, laughing and with tears in her eyes," Few people can imagine that I choose my life. I would have no other life. It is a gift what I have and a gift what I don't have." Today I understand this and am grateful for our family's life, exactly as it is.

The past few years I have seen more communities welcome people who are marginalized into the community and recognize that inclusion changes their community for the better. Often, these people have said to me, "We started out to help people, and then realized we are building a good community for everyone." Finding diversity and difference significant and valuable rather than devalued changes the community for the better for everyone. We all open new possibilities together through inclusion.

> **If I am not who you think I am, then you are not who you thought you are.**
>
> **–James Baldwin**

I want to spend the rest of whatever life I am given working for more opportunities for people who are marginalized, disconnected, isolated, and invisible to enter community fully as contributing citizens. The more people whose gifts are invisible get to contribute as citizens the better for them and the more communities are transformed into places good for us all. When people get in on the blessing of contribution, hearing "we need you", the circle of blessing grows for us all with new life and new energy.

Pied Beauty
Gerard Manley Hopkins, s.J.

Glory be to God for dappled things-
  For skies of couple-colour as a brindled cow;
  For rose-moles all in stipple upon trout that swim;
Fresh-firecoal chestnut-falls; finches' wings;
  Landscape plotted and pieced -fold, fallow, and plough;
And all trades, their gear and tackle and trim.

All things counter, original, spare, strange;
  Whatever is fickle, freckled (who knows how?)
  With swift, slow; sweet, sour; adazzle, dim;
He fathers-forth whose beauty is past change:
  Praise him.

Lessons From the Future

Giving myself the gift of time for reflection and critical thinking has brought me new questions. I have become fascinated to find ways to move deeper into the geometry lesson presented in Chapter 2. The distinction between circles and triangles as forms of organization remains a valid and useful one, but it has grown clearer to me that some of the social inventions we need must take us beyond circles and triangles into new kinds of connection organizations.

One place that this has become clear to me is in my work with organizations whose mission is to support people with disabilities to participate in their communities as full citizens. It seems that developing real community —which is what is wanted outside the organization— can't happen unless the organization itself is living community and not acting like a machine. Rich Crocker, a good friend who has been the director of a large agency that serves people with developmental disabilities, said, "I now realize that if dreams are not real inside my agency then dreams can't be supported for people outside. We have to make it real inside too —where people who work here know their dreams can matter and be taken seriously." Groups of people across all parts of the world are transforming local institutions from conventional triangles into something new, more circle-like, and yet to be named. These usually small transformed triangles have features of stable institutions while also having the life and energy of something living. This process of invention has just started and I know I will be part of it.

A Question for You

A consumer society or a citizen society —which will it be?

Whether the shift to a citizen-centered society happens will be a story told by ordinary people who have the courage and conviction to lead the many changes necessary to promote citizenship for all. Many things threaten this possibility. But the great hope is people like you, whose interest in building community assets led you to read this book.

Throughout the world everyday people, like us, claim the courage to act. Some champions for change lead agencies, some work in the gap between agencies and community residents, some work on the edge of agencies, some are organizers in communities, and some are community residents and association leaders. The great joy of this work is seeing and meeting other people who are also champions for asset based community development. Together we can invent new possibilities for democracy that is real and for citizenship that works. As your encounter with this book ends, remember how we started. We are all together on a road which we create as we walk it. May you enjoy the journey, the friendships along the way, the meaning shared in learning and in contribution together.

One Last Exercise

Five Basic Questions For You

Give yourself at least an hour in a place that supports you to reflect. However it works best for you, reflect deeply on these simple questions. Write down or draw as much as will help you to gain from this reflection and remember its fruits.

- What do I really want to do with my work and with my life?
- Who else do I know on a similar path in my local community? Outside where I live?
- How could we support each other and celebrate each other?
- What resources do I need?
- How might I get what I need?

Use this space to summarize your response to the five basic questions in words and images.

Appendix A
Regenerating Community: The Recovery of a Space for Citizens[1]

John L. McKnight

The Center for Urban Affairs, now renamed the Institute for Policy Research, was founded in 1968. Because I am the only remaining staff member of the founding group, it seems appropriate at this time to report on the beginnings of the Institute's Community Studies Program because of its unusual, perhaps unique, character.

When the Institute began in the throes of the 60s revolution, the spirit of reform was everywhere and it was especially intense among the young people at universities. The Institute's newly assembled faculty was also imbued with this spirit of reform, deeply committed to research that would change American cities that were then sites of revolt, burning, and uprising.

Our initial focus was upon what we called "institutional change." By that we meant better schools, better medical systems, better social service systems, better government, better criminal justice systems, etc. We also assumed that the key to reforming these systems was adequate funding and the introduction of modem technology, personnel training, and management methods. If these kinds of reforms were accomplished, we believed that cities would become livable and residents would thrive. Therefore, our research began with a focus on how modem methods could change the well-being of city people-especially those with lower incomes.

Presented at Northwestern University, 29 May 2003, in the Institute for Policy Research Distinguished Public Policy Lecture Series

[1]By citizen, I do not infer a legal category. Rather, it is a term of power defining a local participant in a democracy.

Shortly after we began our work we initiated a monthly seminar in which all of the Institute's faculty took part in a discussion with an outside expert. The first of our seminar visitors was a well-known physician who was the medical director of the recently formed national Head Start Program. His name was Dr. Robert Mendelsohn. He joined our seminar and quickly learned of our commitment to health through institutional reform of medical systems and hospitals. He reacted with amazement at our institutional focus and said it was unscientific. The great preponderance of the scientific evidence, he explained, indicated that the critical determinants of health were not medical systems or access to them. Therefore, he said, our primary focus on medical system reform was a misguided effort if we were concerned about the health of neighborhood residents. Indeed, he said, we were caught in the "institutional assumption" -the idea that health was produced by hospitals, doctors, and medical systems.

We quickly checked the epidemiological literature and found near unanimity among health researchers supporting Dr. Mendelsohn's claim. It was clear from this research that the four primary determinants of health were individual behavior, social relationships, the physical environment, and economic status. Access to medical systems was not even in the scientific list of primary health determinants. Nor did medical systems have much potential to affect the basic health determinants. Therefore, we would have to do our analyses and research outside of medical systems if we were to join in serious efforts to change individual behavior, social relationships, and the physical and economic environments that determined health.

This faculty experience led some of us to adopt a new intellectual focus and that group became the Community Studies Program. We agreed that we should *not* begin with the "institutional assumption" that held that hospitals produced health, schools produced wisdom, legal systems created justice, social service systems produced social well-being, etc. Instead, we decided to initially focus on the positive conditions of a good life: health, wisdom, justice, community, knowledge, and economic well-being. We decided to examine the scientific evidence regarding the critical determinants of each of *these* conditions.

Once we began this new exploration of the determinants of well-being, we found that the health example was a "generalizable" model. There was clear evidence that school is not the primary source of wisdom or knowledge; social service systems are not major factors in community social well-being; and clearly, criminal justice systems and lawyers are not the primary determinants of safety or justice. In each area, the evidence pointed us in other directions as we focused on the basic determinants of community well-being.

Our inquiry then began anew, and we gathered evidence regarding the primary determinants of well-being in urban neighborhoods. Interestingly enough, the list of health determinants seemed to apply to other areas of well-being as well. The scientific evidence seemed to support the general proposition that the primary determinants of social and economic well-being, safety and justice, wisdom and knowledge, as well as health, were summarized by what happens in terms of individual behavior, social relationships, the physical environment, and economic status.

This realization led us to an understanding that we had been using an inaccurate "map" of society when we followed the "institutional assumption." Our "map" had assumed that personal and community well-being was produced by institutional systems. This assumption inevitably led to a research focus on management, technology, and funding. And of greatest importance, it led to a de-facto classification of local residents as clients-the recipients of institutional services.

Our unrecognized premise was that well-being was determined by the sum of a resident's consumption of services. But could service consumption by clients really change individual behavior, social relationships, the physical and economic environment? Was there any place on the map for the residents and their own actions? Where did citizens and their collective relationships fit in affecting the determinants?

It was at this point, of course, that we recognized that the hidden consequence of the "institutional assumption" is that it creates a social map of systems and clients, while omitting communities and citizens. And yet, it is clear that citizens and their communities must have a major role on the social map if individual behavior, social relations, and the physical and economic environment are to be changed. In fact, many of today's more enlightened institutional leaders have come to adopt this revised map, recognizing the critical role of citizens and their collective work in addition to the institutional functions. For example, most superintendents of police departments now emphasize the importance of local citizen organizations, block watches, and community policing. They are clear that the police and the criminal justice system are extremely limited, at best, in their capacity to deliver safety, security, or justice.

Informed health system administrators increasingly support community health promotion efforts, and many school administrators are recognizing how important parents and local residents are in raising effective young people.

A new map has now emerged in many sectors. It places citizens at the center, surrounded by their social relationships in local groups, clubs, and organizations, supported by a group of local institutions. This is a citizen-centered-rather than a client-centered-map. It recognizes that citizens and their collective relationships are the principal tools for affecting the basic determinants of well-being.

As we proceeded beyond the institutional assumption, it was suggested that we should focus, instead, on civil society. The basic definition of civil society is peculiar because it is usually stated in the negative: It is not the state (government), and it is not the market (for profit business). It is, however, everything else. And two kinds of organizations are located in this space for "everything else." In taking the example of Evanston, Ill., we find first, non-profit groups such as Northwestern University, many hospitals, and social service systems, and second, civic associations such as Rotary Clubs, Alcoholics Anonymous, and local block clubs.

We found that a focus on this definition of civil society was misleading, at least, and counterproductive, at worst. The reason is clear. Incorporated within this same sector, as though they are somehow specially related, are Northwestern University and the Alcoholics Anonymous groups in Evanston-or St. Francis Hospital and the local Rotary Club. The contradiction is obvious. Northwestern University and St. Francis Hospital are large institutions run by paid employees. Alcoholics Anonymous and the Rotary Club are small groups of unpaid citizens working in associations. Therefore, civil society as a working category misled us because it placed the very institutions that we initially wanted to avoid in the same space as local associations-the focus of citizen initiatives.

Indeed, we soon realized that the traditional definition of civil society was dysfunctional because the nonprofit hospital and university are much more like government and business institutions than they are similar to citizens' associations. Northwestern University is basically like the University of Illinois even though one is nonprofit and the other is a governmental institution. It is, on the other hand, radically different from Alcoholics Anonymous. Similarly, St. Francis Hospital is very like a for-profit Humana Hospital and very unlike a Rotary Club.

Therefore, we found it essential in our analysis to distinguish between nonprofit institutions and local citizen associations if we were to understand the basic determinants of well-being and avoid the institutional assumption. We abandoned civil society as a useful category and re-classified nonprofit systems with the other systems of the state and the market. We focused instead on the citizen sector of associational life to understand it as a potential community resource for change in individual behavior, social relations, the physical environment, and economic status

The associational sector is that social space where citizens join in face-to-face groups and do their work without pay as members of a voluntary association of citizens.[2] These groups are incredibly diverse in their concerns and forms. They include Alcoholics Anonymous, Rotary Clubs, choirs, religious organizations, sports leagues, social cause groups, women's associations, block clubs, motorcycle clubs, etc.

Alexis de Tocqueville was the first to define these groups. Writing in 1834 in what would become *Democracy in America,* his brilliant analysis of the developing structure of America's society, he said:

> Americans of all ages, all conditions, and all dispositions constantly form
> associations. They have not only commercial and manufacturing companies,
> in which all take part, but associations of a thousand other kinds, religious,

---

2 An association may have a paid member (pastor, organizer, secretary), but unpaid citizen members do the essential work.

moral, serious, futile, general or restricted, enormous or diminutive. The
Americans make associations to give entertainment, to found seminaries,
to build inns, to construct churches, to diffuse books, to send missionaries
to the antipodes; in this manner they found hospitals, prisons, and schools.
If it is proposed to inculcate some truth or to foster some feeling by the en-
couragement of a great example, they form a society. Wherever at the head
of some new undertaking you see the government in France, or a man of rank
in England, in the United States you will be sure to find an association.[3]

Nothing, in my opinion, is more deserving of our attention than the intel-
lectual and moral associations of America. The political and industrial
associations of that country strike us forcibly; but the others (the civic
associations) elude our observations, or if we discover them, we understand
them imperfectly because we have hardly ever seen anything of the kind. It
must be acknowledged, however, that they are as necessary to the Ameri-
can people as the former (industrial and governmental associations), and
perhaps more so. In democratic countries the science of association is the
mother of science; the progress of all the rest depends upon the progress it
has made.[4]

Tocqueville was pointing out that in associations of whatever kind, Americans were inventing a unique context for cooperative, creative action that engaged the individual citizen in *producing society, reshaping social relations* in ways too diverse to enumerate, *transforming the environment* (for good and ill) and creating the *context for entrepreneurship.* He classified all of this activity in political terms. For him, every person in an association of any kind was a citizen at work rather than a client, consumer, or even constituent. Indeed, he recognized that while the citizen as voter is essential, voting is actually a process of giving power away-the delegation of authority. In association, however, the American was, in concert with fellow citizens, making power. He saw that, in associations, Americans became producers of well-being rather than recipients of institutional favors-that their essential tool for creating effective communities was their associations.

This new form of associative citizen power was so revolutionary that his book's title attempts to point out that there is a new kind of *Democracy In America*-the associational community where citizens went beyond voting and

---

3 Alexis de Tocqueville, *Democracy in America* (New York: Vintage Books, vol. 2, 1945), 114.
4 Ibid, 118.

created a new form of relationships to make power and create a society from their own vision and work

For these reasons, we decided that viewing the urban neighborhood through its associational life could provide a context for understanding how the basic determinants of well-being are affected, changed, and created. In this way we would not be starting with the institutional assumption. We would be starting with the citizen-centered, rather than the system-client-consumer, map.

Because our colleague Robert Putnam's book, *Bowling Alone*,[5] has become so well known with its dismal analysis of the decline of American associational life, it is reasonable to ask whether a focus on associational life is relevant anymore. Has the citizen centered society atrophied, replaced by institutional systems meeting every need of a supine society of consumers and clients?

The answer is that it depends upon where you look. If you look in newly built tract suburbs, for example, the map of associational life is largely vacant. If you look in older, inner-city neighborhoods, the map is quite different.

Our research has discovered, in city after city, a rich associational framework in these older neighborhoods. In Chicago's mid-south neighborhood of Grand Boulevard, one of its very lowest in income, a neighborhood inventory found 319 voluntary associations.[6] In Chicago's Westside Austin neighborhood, 612 associations were counted.[7] In each case, the research was focused on associations with names and did not include those hundreds of associational groups that gather without the formality of a name.

Having assisted many neighborhood groups in associational inventories, we can identify the common forms of associational life in these neighborhoods. The typology shows the kinds of groups commonly created by citizens in inner city neighborhoods:

While it is obvious by their names that many of these groups provide great

---

5 Robert Putnam, *Bowling Alone*. New York: Simon & Schuster, 2000

6 John McKnight, John Kretzmann, and Nicol Turner, *Voluntary Associations in Low-Income Neighborhoods: An Unexplored Community Resource* (IPR Working Paper Series: Program on Community Development, 1996), p. 4

7 John McKnight and John Kretzmann, A *Guide to Mapping and Mobilizing the Associations in Local Neighborhoods,* (Chicago: ACTA Publications, 1999) p. 34

Master List of Associations

Addiction Prevention & Recovery Groups
- Drug ministries/ Testimonial groups for addicts
- Campaigns for drug-free neighborhood
- High school substance abuse committees.

Advisory Community Support Groups (Friends of…)
- Friends of the library
- Neighborhood park advisory
- Hospital advisory

Animal Care Groups
- Cat owners' association
- Humane Society

Anti-Crime Groups
- Children's Safe Haven neighborhood group
- Police Neighborhood Watch
- Senior safety group

Block Clubs
- Condominium associations
- Building councils
- Tenant Clubs

Business Organizations/ Support Groups
- Jaycees
- Chamber of Commerce (local)
- Economic Development Councils
- Restaurant Associations

Charitable Groups & Drives
- Hospital auxiliaries (local)
- United Way (local)

Civic Events Groups
- Parade planning committees
- Arts & crafts fairs
- July 4th Carnival Committee
- Health fair committees

Cultural Groups
- Community Choirs
- Drama groups
- High school bands

Disability Groups
- Special Olympics
- American Lung Association
- Muscular Dystrophy Association

Education Groups
- School Councils
- Book clubs
- Parent-Teacher Associations
- Tutoring groups

Elderly Groups
- Hospital senior's clubs
- Church senior's clubs
- Senior crafts clubs

Environmental Groups
- Adopt-a-stream
- Bike path committee
- Clean-air committee
- Save the park group

Family Support Groups
- Parent alliance groups
- Foster Parent support groups

Health & Fitness
- TOPS
- Neighborhood health council
- Fitness groups
- Yoga clubs

Heritage Groups
- Black empowerment groups
- Norwegian society
- Neighborhood historical society

Hobby & Collectors
- Antique collectors clubs
- Stamp & coin collectors clubs
- Garden club
- Sewing club

Men's Groups
- Fraternal orders
- Men's sports groups

Mentoring Groups
- Peer mentors
- Big Brother/ Big Sister
- After-school mentors

Mutual Support Groups
- La Leche League
- Disease support groups
- Parenting Groups

Neighborhood Improvement
- Council of block clubs
- Neighborhood clean-up

Political Organizations
- Democrat & Republican clubs
- League of women voters

Recreation
- Bowling leagues
- Basketball leagues
- Little league
- * Motorcycle clubs

Religious Groups
- Churches, mosques, & synagogues & affiliated groups
- Inter-faith initiatives

Service Clubs
- Rotary
- Zonta International

Social Groups
- Card playing groups
- * Social Activity Clubs

Social Cause Advocacy
- Community action councils
- Hunger organizations

Unions
- Industrial
- Craft

Veteran's Groups
- American legion
- VFW

Women's Groups
- Women's institute groups
- Women's sports groups

Youth Groups
- Scouts
- Boys & Girls Clubs
- Junior Achievement

community benefit, our research also indicates that these groups engage in many activities that benefit the community even though their names do not suggest the breadth of their community work. For example, a baseball team keeps up the neighborhood park where they play; the church creates an after-school program for all local teens; the motorcycle club's clubhouse is the meeting place for the neighborhood association; the neighborhood association is part of a national lobby to change discriminatory banking practices; four local associations create a new neighborhood economic development group to join the local businesses in reviving the commercial strip; a local women's organization creates a constructive summer initiative for the girls in the neighborhood; a group of local men's associations create a neighborhood watch program in which their members patrol the local community evenings; a senior's club visits homebound seniors, delivers meals and calls each homebound senior every day; an association of block clubs confronts a local employer about its discriminatory employment practices; an association of young people interviews local seniors and writes a neighborhood history; a local association of associations envisions and creates an initiative to rehabilitate neighborhood apartment buildings; a veteran's organization creates a job training program; an association of local churches collaborates with the local school to create a youth reading program; and on and on. The generally undocumented, unsupported, and uncelebrated community benefits of local associations is the untold story of the continuing inventions of inner-city citizen associations and their community-building capacities, even in the 21st century.

Here we must recognize the pernicious effects of racial and ethnic discrimination in the American story. These effects are the rock upon which the American ship has so often floundered. Race has been the means for pervasive economic exploitation of neighborhoods, their people, and their housing. Nonetheless, associational life has been a powerful defense and offense against segregation and discrimination. Historically, churches, temples, and mosques have been bulwarks for neighbors of differing racial and ethnic backgrounds. The great African-American scholars St. Clair Drake and W.E.B. DuBois both identify the urban associations of black people as the principal means for their survival and ascendance. Perhaps this is why we have found such numerous and diverse associations within low-income communities, for among those who our institutions have often ignored or exploited, it would seem quite reasonable that the associational alternative would remain a vigorous and vital local resource. Therefore, in spite of the reported decline of associations, our research indicates that they remain quite numerous in low-income communities. Their survival is obviously essential, for they perform unique functions that elude the great professions and institutions of our society.

While I have written elsewhere of the numerous unique functions of associations,[8] here I would like to emphasize those functions that seem most significant in achieving neighborhoods where health, wisdom, justice, knowledge, economic well-being, and community prevail.

At the heart of the democratic faith is an idea that reaches beyond equality. It is the idea that every person has unique skills, capacities, and gifts and that a good society provides an opportunity for those gifts to be given and shared. In this way the community grows strong because each person provides unique contributions to the common good so that the sum of the parts is a free, productive neighborhood. In this sense, associations are a democratic society's primary vehicle for identifying, combining, and manifesting the unique gifts of citizens for the common good. An association is the structure we have uniquely created to provide a means of coalescing the capacities of each to create a synthesis, making each participant more powerful and the group's power greater than the individual power of each member. In this synthesis, we can see why Tocqueville felt associations were Americans' democratic tool for making power. Or in more contemporary language, why the basic site of "empowerment" resides in association rather than in a client or a consumer.

In addition to being a principal means for citizens to be powerful and create power, associations provide a vital resource for creative problem-solving. In the diversity of citizen experience within each association and the diversity of purposes in a neighborhood's associations, the "raw material" for creative solutions to questions large and small is generated. Indeed, most of our old systems, agencies, enterprises, and institutions were hatched in the associational "nest." The critical question today is whether we can recognize what Tocqueville saw so well- that the place where new solutions to basic dilemmas will be generated is in associational life.

---

8 John McKnight, *Careless Society* (New York: Basic Books), 161.

Unfortunately, we spend so much of our effort, attention, and resources on institutional reform that we usually ignore the inventive-and often more effective-efforts of citizens in associations as they grapple with the questions of neighborhood change. In our book, *Building Communities from the Inside Out*, we document hundreds of creative local initiatives in which associations of local citizens are inventing, creating, and discovering new paths for raising young people, revitalizing their economy, overcoming discrimination, promoting health, and ensuring security.[9] These efforts, however, fall largely under the radar of most researchers, marketers, governments, funders, and the media. Nonetheless, citizens are persistently at work creating new ways to meet those human needs resulting from the inherent limits of large institutions and systems.

One other irreplaceable attribute of associational life is care. Many neighborhoods are recipients of institutional services that are mistakenly called care. There are health care, care providers, systems of care, Medicare, "judicare." Each is a system providing a paid *service* but structurally unable to produce care.

Care is the freely given commitment from the heart of one to another. No system can mandate, manage, produce, or provide this kind of care. A university can manage to provide students a service called education. However, it cannot manage professors so that they will care for their students. Some faculty *might* care, but no president, provost, dean, or chair can make the university produce care for students.

Most of our institutions compete in creating the illusion that their service is really care. The telephone company advertises that it cares about you, the insurance company will care for you, the government will show it cares for you, and even your undertaker will care for you-if posthumously.

The point is that bureaucratic systems are attempting to graft onto themselves the primary characteristics of voluntary associations. Unlike institutions, associations are structures in which care is central. People voluntarily join together because they *care* about one another, and they *care* about some

---

9 John McKnight and John Kretzmann, *Building Communities from the Inside Out* (Chicago: ACTA Publications, 1993).

common purpose or cause. This care is from the heart, freely given, a *voluntary* commitment to the other, and a common *vision*.

It is one of the quiet tragedies of the 20th century that we have accepted the idea that institutions, rather than families, neighbors, and associations, are the primary sites of care. This mistaken understanding is the cause, rather than the solution, of many of our social problems. Who among us looks forward to old age under the "care" of a nursing home, now called a "care" facility? And what young person surrounded by professional "servicers" -educational, recreational, psychological, correctional-is aware that these professionals are creating a counterfeit community that can never replace the concern, insight, experience, support, and love of a genuine community of care?

The critical reasons, then, for recognizing the place of associations in our local neighborhoods and larger society is that they are our citizen tools for creating power, inventing solutions, and providing care. And these are the three capacities that our great systems cannot produce, however well managed, technologically oriented, or professionally run.

The focus of this lecture is to consider questions of policy. In terms of associational life, there is an obvious paradox. Practically speaking, policy is a word that usually applies to institutions and their intentions rather than associations and their commitments. Policies are adopted by corporations, nonprofit institutions, and governments. And as we have seen, it is their policies that have been major factors in the decline of associational life even though these policies have been understood by the institutions as being helpful, meeting "needs," and fulfilling demand. Paradoxically, policies suggesting more of these interventions would obviously be counterproductive.

We are faced with an unusual dilemma. What institutional policy could allow or support the growth of associational space and citizen action?

One approach to this question is the possibility that local institutions could be support structures for associational life. Indeed, their language suggests support rather than control, or even partnership. They often describe themselves as servants-civil servants, public servants, and servants providing health, social, economic, and cultural services. How can they transform themselves from being lords of institutional intervention into servants of citizens and their associations?

It is possible to describe many institutional polices that support associational life, and we have done so in our book *Building Communities from the Inside Out*. It may be more useful, however, to describe the actual policy of one unusual institution that took seriously the question of how it might become a servant of the associational community. This particular example recounts a recent policy change made by the Atlanta Metropolitan United Way.

The United Way has traditionally been an institution supporting increased intervention by human service systems in all aspects of community life. It has been a major contributor to the policy map that defines local neighborhoods and their residents as needy, problem-filled places to be "fixed" by professionally provided services. Therefore, it is startling-and exemplary-to find a local United Way supporting an increased space for citizen, associational, and community creativity, and problem solving.

The following policy proposal-comparing the existing and proposed replacement policies-of the Atlanta United Way was presented to its board:

The New Policy: Community Building

Present Policy	Proposed New Policy
Focus on **deficiencies**	Focus on **assets**
Problem response	Opportunity identification
Charity orientation	Investment orientation
Grants to agencies	Grants, loans, investments, leveraging dollars
More services	Fewer services
High emphasis on agencies	Emphasis on associations, businesses, agencies, churches
Focus on individuals	Focus on communities/ neighborhoods
Maintenance	Development
See people as **clients**	See people as **citizens**
"Fix" people	Develop potential
Programs are the answer	People are the answer

The board of the Atlanta United Way voted 69-0 to implement the new policy.

This policy change implicitly recognizes that the essential institutional policy for regenerating community is to create a space for the citizen center to grow. Henry Moore, the brilliant assistant manager of Savannah, GA, described his city's uniquely successful neighborhood renewal policy as "leading by stepping back." It is a policy that shifts from prescription to proscription, from "How we will fix them" to "What we won't do to limit them."

I am sure that this idea of policies that focus on institutional limits and "stepping back" is not what most institutional and professional policy leaders are looking for. What a letdown for a policy forum! Americans, however, have a great policy precedent for recognizing institutional limits. It was, after all, the people who instituted our government who invented an institution and then, understanding the importance of limits, created a list of proscriptions on the very institution they newly created. We call those proscriptions our Bill of Rights. And the first of those proscriptions says that the government may not limit freedom of speech and association.

There remains the question of whether the very idea of policy can be focused on associations themselves. Who would have the authority or capacity to prescribe or implement an associational policy for citizens In local neighborhoods? The essence of our freedom in this democracy is the fact that no one *can* create a policy for citizens in their voluntary associations. Indeed, it is the essence of a totalitarian society that its policy is that *every* association must serve the system. So, instead of the Girl or Boy Scouts, there would be Hitler's Youth or the Young Patriots.

Let us recognize, then, that we are opposed to a policy for American associational life because we seek to be a free people. And it is our control of this citizen space that is the source of our power, our creativity, our care, and our democracy.

There is, however, a way to measure the power of our citizens in association. There are four indicators of whether we have the citizen assets to lead our democracy ahead.

The first is the power to create the **vision** for our future. This means that we are not the advisors or even partners of institutional visionaries. We are the fountainhead from which our destiny must flow.

The second is that we are the principal **producers** of our destiny. As citizens we have heads *and* hands. We are not dependent on institutions to carry out our vision. We can imagine and produce our future with institutions as our assistants.

The third power is our ability to act as the **connectors** of assets-the catalyst of relationships. Community building is basically about understanding our neighborhood assets and creating new connections among them. But we must be the connectors, for when institutions perform these functions, we become wholly owned subsidiaries, mere objects of and participants in their programs.

Lastly, and of greatest importance, is our **power to care**. Care is the name we give to a powerful relationship:

"I care about them."

"I will *care* for him through his dying days."

"I care about this neighborhood."

"I care about our youth."

These "cares" are the powerful source of associational life. For, in voluntary associations we are not motivated by money. The force at the citizen center, the force that holds us together, is care.

Let us remember that care does not come from managers, systems, professions, institutions, or computers. Care comes from the heart of citizens, and its public expression is through our associations.

Tocqueville saw this clearly. He wondered how these New World citizens in local places were guided in creating their new, unique, and unprecedented associations. He concluded that they knew how to create this unique new democracy because they followed the "habits of the heart."

It is these "habits" that have persevered and have provided the foundation of our democracy. What a privilege it is to have our powers of association. What a glory to have the power to care. What a responsibility to be a citizen. For we are the dreamers of democracy, we are the architects, the builders, and the residents of the American dream. And that is not so wild a dream.

Appendix B
Community Building in Freemont
Lynn Ross and Henry Moore

The City of Fremont, California is a community of assets. This city is home to a thriving business community, largely represented by the industrial, manufacturing, biotechnology and technology sectors. Fremont is a Silicon Valley community with over 1,200 high-tech firms. Fremont is home to more than just a strong business community; this is also a community comprised of a diverse, young, and well-educated citizenry. Lead by a progressive local government, the city was honored in 1997 as an "All America City."

Rich in history and culture, Fremont is clearly a dynamic community. What really makes this community tick, however, are not its individual assets. Rather, it is how those assets- government, business, and citizens- come together that truly make Fremont an interesting community to learn from.

Community Profile

Brief History

In 1956, the California towns of Warm Springs, Mission San Jose, Centerville, Niles and Irvington incorporated to become one city --Fremont. Previously, the area was unincorporated land under the jurisdiction of the Alameda County Board of Supervisors. At that time of incorporation, Fremont was comprised over almost 100 square miles and had a population of approximately 22,000. Not surprisingly, melding together five separate towns with five separate identities to form a single, unified city was not without challenges. The controversy surrounding the decisions of where to locate the city center, including the city hall and other governmental services, further entrenched feelings of division within the new city. However, the creation of a locally controlled government, centralized planning structure, and community growth strategy helped to create a sense of city identity among Fremont's residents.

Demographics

Today, Fremont (population 209,000) is the fourth largest city in the San Francisco Bay Area. Located within the Silicon Valley, the city covers a land area of over 90 square miles and is home to a diverse population: 41% White, 37% Asian, 14% Latino, 3% African American, 4% two or more races. Like the city itself, the residents of Fremont are relatively young. In fact, over 70% of the population is under the age of 45. Residents over the age of 55 comprise just 16% of the population. Average household income is approximately $107,000. Forty-two percent of Fremont households have an annual income upwards of $100,000; whereas, just over 20% percent of the households have an average annual income of $50,000 or less. Based on these income levels, it is no surprise to find that almost half of the residents have completed at least a college degree.

The Community Building and Engagement Initiative

The Community Building and Engagement Initiative was born out of a series of focus group and public meetings hosted by the city from October 2000 through January 2001. From October to December 2000, some 200 Fremont residents participated in 20 focus groups along with city staff. The purpose of these focus groups was to examine current civic engagement practices as well as consider additional strategies for building community.

In January 2001, 60 residents met with staff to review the focus group findings and come to a consensus on proposed strategies. Meeting attendees also reviewed a set of draft community engagement strategies created by city staff. The original strategies included:

- Organizing neighborhood networks;
- Considering an expanded agenda;
- Establishing City-Neighborhood Liaisons;
- Providing leadership training;
- Establishing a resource library;
- Sponsoring an annual community meeting;
- Establishing a community engagement newsletter;

- Expanding service learning; and

- Wiring Fremont for community engagement.

The Community Building and Engagement Plan

These strategies along with a list of related City Council priorities formed the basis for the Community Building and Engagement Plan. The plan centers around four broad goals:

Goal 1. Strengthen community engagement efforts at the block, neighborhood, and citywide levels.

Goal 2. Build community and staff capacity for community engagement.

Goal 3. In collaboration with FUSD [Fremont Unified School District], strengthen youth service learning.

Goal 4. Encourage the use of the internet as a tool to strengthen community engagement.

About Goal 1

The city had an existing core of block-level organizations in the form of neighborhood watch, homeowners associations, school organizations, etc. The goal of the plan is to strengthen these existing organizations while creating opportunities for leaders to come together at varying levels to create new networks. The plan outlined a variety of strategies to achieve this goal, including expanding the numbers of activities, creating neighborhood networks, establishing city liaisons, and holding annual citywide community engagement summit's.

About Goal 2

The city felt it should have a key role in building the capacity of both its staff and residents in terms of community engagement. Strategies to address this goal included the creation of a resource library that would offer those interested access to materials on community building, organizing and outreach tools. Another strategy was to provide community engagement training to city staff and to community leaders. The final strategy involved creating a community engagement newsletter that would highlight civic efforts across Fremont.

About Goal 3

This goal required working with the Fremont Unified School District to expand on their existing service-learning efforts. The purpose of this focus on service-learning was to engage the youth of Fremont with the community and foster a sense of civic responsibility. The primary strategy associated with this goal was the creation of a Service-Learning Partnership. The partnership would be comprised of FUSD representatives, city staff, teachers, students, nonprofits and others who would help to identify service-learning projects as well as handle issues of funding, liability, outreach and transportation.

About Goal 4

Given Fremont's standing as a high-tech community, this goal was designed to take advantage of the many technologies available which enable broader engagement. Strategies included a redesign of the city website and use of electronic communication by the city to reach more citizens.

Although increased collaboration among city staff and departments was required, implementation of the plan was designed to use existing resources. The plan is administered by the Office of Neighborhoods and the Police Department.

Stakeholder Perspectives

In preparation for writing this case, a series of brief interviews were conducted with local government officials, city staff and residents. The following provides a summary of the key points offered by each group:

- Local government can not (and should not) do it all. Citizens have a responsibility too. (Local Government Officials, Citizens, City Staff)
- Engagement efforts are challenged by the physical layout of the city. The city is spread out and residents are just becoming accustomed to neighborhood boundaries. These factors make coming together difficult. (Citizens, City Staff)
- The staff really has to be trained in order to effectively implement this initiative. (Local Government Officials, Citizens)
- The government can still do more to reach out to citizens. (Citizens)

The philosophy behind the Community Building and Engagement Initiative actually has its origins in the formation of the city itself. Just as the five original towns decided to work together to form one community, the local government decided to work with its citizenry to strengthen that same community. The success of the Community Building and Engagement Initiative is difficult to measure at this point. However, this table illustrates the few quantifiable measure of success currently available for the initiative.

	Years					
	97-98	98-99	99-00	00-01	01-02	02-03
Indicators						
Staff	1	1	6	6 + 2 interns	8 + 3 interns	6
Budget	Unavailable					$565,000
Summit Attendees	NA			350	475	
Database	NA			3,500	5,000	6,000
Neighborhood Crime Watch Groups	Unavailable			450	575	600
Trained residents	NA			420	510	255
CERT members	0	0	0	0	2100	2800
NNO						
· # of parties	NA	47	72	87	101	121
· # of people		940	1585	2165	2727	3630
Email groups	NA			0	0	16
Neighborhood Networks	NA			0	0	16
Leaders	NA			0	0	0

Source: City of Fremont, Office of Neighborhoods

Fremont is already experiencing some of the benefits of an engaged citizenry. The statistics demonstrate increased participation and a growing staff and budget, but there are additional benefits the city may experience over time. First, the ability to attract private sector investment will be enhanced. Banks are generally more willing to invest when they see a history of citizens working to protect neighborhoods. Second, the ability to build citizen momentum the physical redevelopment of the neighborhood will improve. As Fremont citizens continue to work together in their neighborhoods, for their neighborhoods they are more likely to act as catalyst for housing development, neighborhood growth and revitalization efforts.

The initiative is just over two years old and, therefore, it is difficult to ascertain the success of the initiative at this early stage. The truest measure of its success will be the lasting relationships and networks created between city and residents as well as among residents.

Lessons

Fremont's local government seemingly operates with three guiding principles for civic engagement:

- Institutions as servants.

- Every citizen has a gift.

- Citizen-centered organizations are the key to community partnerships.

It is this set of guiding principles that provide the general lessons for this case study.

Institutions as Servants

City government can be of invaluable help supporting the work of citizens' initiatives to engage their members. Fremont's leaders recognized that there were limits to what government could do for neighborhoods as a result of budget reductions and staff capacity. Further, the city understood the importance of asking citizens about their concerns, listening for their answer and responding with a bottom-up approach that involved citizens in the decision-making.

Every Citizen has a Gift

There is unrecognized capacity in every community. Citizen gifts and talents must be supported and nurtured because citizens can and want to contribute to the improvement of their community. Fremont city leaders recognized that an involved citizenry would improve neighborhood appearance, safety and overall community well-being. The city takes great pride in its diverse population and the many gifts this population has to offer. The community responds with appreciation for the city's support by remaining engaged.

Citizen-centered Organizations are the Key to Community Partnerships

Engaging neighborhood leaders is a strong leadership development tool for neighborhoods. It is an asset based approach that recognizes the power of building relationships and strengthening local associations. However, community partnerships rarely emerge without intentional relationship building. Fremont hired a community organizer to lead its Office of Neighborhoods and to foster community power by building relationships. The organizer was given a free hand to mobilize the community and her success is evidenced by the continuous increase in citizen participation and neighborhood group formation.

Summary

The Community Building and Engagement Initiative is still in its infancy, but the underlying principles of the initiative have been a part of the fabric in Fremont for some time. The initiative and its implementation plan provide a solid framework for every stakeholder to work from. Fremont demonstrates that when strong guiding principles come together with strong implementation tools in an environment of civic engagement, the community and its people can be strengthened.

The City of Fremont website   http://www.fremont.gov

FremontOnline   http://www.fremontonline.org

Resources

Asset Based Community Development (ABCD)

ABCD Institute www.northwestern.edu/ipr/abcd.html offers a complete listing with access information of the many ABCD Institute publications at www.northwestern.edu/ipr/abcd/abcdpubs.html including workbooks, articles for download, and a list of articles by John McKnight.

Books

Building Communities from the Inside Out: A Path Toward Finding and Mobilizing a Community's Assets, John. Kretzmann and John McKnight. Chicago, ACTA Publications. (1993).

> The original book of ABCD which first described the ABCD perspective; filled with many stories and examples.

Careless Society: Community and Its Counterfeits, by John McKnight New York: Basic Books (1995)

> If Building Communities From the Inside Out points towards 'what to do', then Careless Society points towards 'what not to do', an analysis of the many ways community is undermined.

Power: Building Community The Seattle Way by Jim Diers, Seattle, University of Washington (2004).

> A practical and inspiring book!

The Power of Asset Mapping: how Your Congregation Can Act on its Gifts by Luther Snow. Herndon, Alban Institute (2004)

> Truly every group has more than they think.

Guides to ABCD practice

A Guide to Mapping and Mobilizing the Economic Capacities of Local Residents, by John Kretzmann, John McKnight, and Deborah Puntenney (1996)

A Guide to Mapping Local Business Assets and Mobilizing Local Business Capacities, by John Kretzmann, John McKnight, and Deborah Puntenney (1996)

A Guide to Mapping Consumer Expenditures and Mobilizing Consumer Expenditure Capacities, by John Kretzmann, John McKnight, and Deborah Puntenney (1996)

A Guide to Capacity Inventories: Mobilizing the Community Skills of Local Residents, by John Kretzmann, John McKnight, and Geralyn Sheehan, with Mike Green and Deborah Puntenney (1997)

A Guide to Evaluating Asset-Based Community Development: Lessons, Challenges, and Opportunities, by Tom Dewar (1997)

A Guide to Creating a Neighborhood Information Exchange: Building Communities by Connecting Local Skills and Knowledge, by John Kretzmann, John Mcknight and Deborah Puntenney (1998)

City-Sponsored Community Building: Savannah's Grants for Blocks Story, by Deborah Puntenney and Henry Moore (1998)

Newspapers and Neighborhoods: Strategies for Achieving Responsible Coverage of Local Communities, edited by John Kretzmann, John McKnight, and Deborah Puntenney (1999)

A Guide to Mapping and Mobilizing the Associations in Local Neighborhoods, by Nicol Turner, John McKnight, and John Kretzmann (1999)

Leading by Stepping Back: A Guide for City Officials on Building Neighborhood Capacity, by Henry Moore and Deborah Puntenney (1999)

A Guide to Building Sustainable Organizations from the Inside Out: An Organizational Capacity Building Toolbox from the Chicago Foundation for Women, by Deborah Puntenney (2000).

The Organization of Hope: A Workbook for Rural Asset-Based Community Development, by Luther Snow (2001)

Community Transformation: Turning Threats into Opportunities, by Luther Snow with the assistance of Uchenna Ukaegbu (2001).

Asset-Based Strategies for Faith Communities, by Susan Rans and Hilary Altman (2002).

Building the Mercado Central: Asset-Based Development and Community Entrepreneurship, by Geralyn Sheehan (2003).

Publications for download from ABCD Institute

Hidden Treasures: Building Community Connections by Engaging the Gifts of people on welfare, people with disabilities, people with mental illness, older adults, and young people, by Susan A. Rans with Mike Green (2005)

Regenerating Community: The Recovery of a Space for Citizens, by John L. McKnight, Distinguished Public Policy Lecture, Institute for Policy Research (2003)

New Community Tools for Improving Child Health: A Pediatrician's Guide to Local Associations, by John L. McKnight and Carol A. Pandak (1999)

Building the Bridge from Client to Citizen: A Community Toolbox for Welfare Reform, by John P. Kretzmann and Mike Green (1998)

A Twenty-First Century Map for Healthy Communities and Families, by John L. McKnight (1997)

Voluntary Associations in Low-Income Neighborhoods: An Unexplored Community Resource, by John P. Kretzmann, John L. McKnight, and Nicol Turner

Community-Based Development and Local Schools: A Promising Partnership,

Community Building in Logan Square, by Mary O'Connell (1993)

The Gift of Hospitality, by Mary O'Connell (1988)

ABCD for Inclusion

Besides ABCD publications there are many other resources, publications, and videos available about connecting and supporting marginalized people to move into community membership. Particularly important is Inclusion Press at www.Inclusion.com with many excellent resources on building community to support a person to walk the road from the edge of the community into community membership in a person centered way. under the direction of the person herself. Many videos, books, and other

resources are available. These five books exemplify this approach.

PATH: Planning Possible Positive Futures by Jack Pearpoint, John O'Brien, Marsha Forest

> PATH is a creative planning tool that starts in the future and works backwards to an outcome of first (beginning) steps that are possible and positive. It is excellent for team building. It has been used to mediate conflicts. PATH is not for the faint of heart. It is very results oriented. It is unique in its focus on the pathfinders dream and vision of the future and the focus on enrolling community allies needed to move towards that future.

Members of Each Other: Building Community in Company with People with Developmental Disabilities by John O'Brien and Connie Lyle O'Brien

> This book exposes the dangers of power, of isolation, of helplessness. It also challenges and gives hope for communities to commit to care for each other.

From Behind the Piano: The Building of Judith Snow's Unique Circle of Friends by Jack Pearpoint and *What's Really Worth Doing And How to Do It A Book for People WhoLove Someone Labeled Disabled* by Judith Snow (Two books in one)

> This "Two in One" book is the story of Judith Snow's life and circle of support. It is also Judith's wisdom from a lifetime of receiving help and support about what is worth doing. A little book with as much good thinking about the art of living as any book that I know.

A Little Book On Person Centered Planning edited by John O'Brien and Connie Lyle O'Brien

> Ways to think about person-centered planning, its limitations, the conditions for its success with John O'Brien and Connie Lyle O'Brien – Editors. A series of essays offering critical thinking about the practical issues of making person centered plans.

Make A Difference: A Guidebook for Person-Centered Direct Support by John O'Brien and Beth Mount with contributions from Peter Leidy and Bruce Blaney

> This very practical book supports action learning about relationship building, planning with people in a person-centered way, supporting choice, and building community inclusion. (Learning Journey workbooks go with the book.) If you want to learn what to do or teach others what to do to support a person in a way that leads to a meaningful life in community, this book offers guidance worth following.

Community Organizing

American Social Change Organizing

Asset Based Community Development (ABCD) and ABCD organizing came out of this tradition.

Rules for Radicals: A Practical Primer for Realistic Radicals. New York: Vintage Books, by Saul Alinsky 1971.

> The founder of American community organizing tells how to achieve real political power for the practice of true democracy.

Roots for Radicals: Organizing for Power, Action, and Justice by Edward Chambers with Michael Cowan. New York: Continuum, 2003.

> Presents a distillation of the Industrial Areas Foundation (IAF) philosophy and its approach to community organizing and encourages reflection about public life and ideals.

Let the People Decide: Neighborhood Organizing in America. Updated Edition by Robert Fisher. New York: Twayne, 1995.

> Insightfully traces the history of neighborhood organizing in the U.S. A valuable resource for those who want to understand social change community organizing in America.

The Democratic Promise: Saul Alinsky and his Legacy. Video. Berkeley: U of CA Extension Center for Media and Independent Learning, (1999) or Independent Television Service, 501 York Street, San Francisco, CA 94110; http://www.itvs.org/.

Popular Education:

Pedagogy of the Oppressed by Paulo Friere New York, New York: Continuum, (2000)

> The power of ordinary people learning together in community to take action to change reality

The Long Haul: An Autobiography by Myles Horton, New York, Teachers College Press,1997

> This book is about the work of developing learning in ways that are truly empowering of others. Read about the ideas and life of Myles Horton - as well as the story of the Highlander Center learning community. Social change will always be a natural outcome of true learning.

New Kinds of Organizing and Social Learning

Many creative approaches to bringing people together in meaningful ways are developing across the world in work organizations and in communities. ABCD organizing is a part of this new kind of organizing. Here are a few resources as a start that will point you to many more resources!

Finding Our Way by Margaret Wheatley, San Francisco, Berrett-Koehler (2005).

> A book which points at the power and possibilities for organizing in communities where people move into more relationship with each other to create new living organizations designed for human beings to be more fully human. Makes sense about 'what is worth doing' to create new possibilities in practical action for change.

Berkana Institute intentionally supports those who are giving birth to the new forms, processes, and leadership that will restore hope to the future. Berkana nurtures and supports leadership for new invention and for social transformation, hosts learning communities, learning journeys, and communities of practice. Founded by Margaret Wheatley. Many wonderful resources, programs, projects, and links for community building. www.berkana.org

Open Space Technology is an approach to organizing large-scale, participative meetings in which diverse groups come together for the purposes of managing complex issues in short periods of time, with no advance agenda, and minimal facilitation. Open Space is widely known for its Four Principles: 1) Whoever comes is the right people, 2) Whatever happens is the only thing that could have, 3) Whenever it starts if the right time, 4) When it's over it's over, and its Law of Two Feet, which allows for movement of participants from discussion to discussion, given their judgment of where they can best learn and contribute. http://www.openspaceworld.org

The World Café, a conversation circle process invented by close friends, Juanita Brown and David Isaacs, now has global reach and users across all sectors. The focus of World Café is on questions that matter, in the belief meaningful questions nourish the networks of conversation upon which the vitality of organizational and community life depends. Website offers a wealth of resources and support for hosting cafes and connecting with others around the world engaged in similar work. www.theworldcafe.com

Appreciative Inquiry is a form of study that seeks to "locate, highlight, and illuminate" what are "life-giving forces" in an organization or community. The underlying theory of Appreciative Inquiry is that as social beings, we construct reality in our organizations and communities based on what we talk about, what we envision together, and what we study. In other words, we bring forth more of whatever it is we pay attention to. If we pay attention to what is life-giving, rather than life-destroying, we will produce more of life. See http://appreciativeinquiry.cwru.edu/

Shambhala Institute For Authentic Leadership is an international network of people, projects, and programs is actively engaged in the organizational and societal challenges of our time. The Institute is based in Halifax, Nova Scotia. The Institute supports, connects, and amplifies the bright lights across organizations and communities—the visionaries, pathfinders, entrepreneurs, and other agents of change and innovation in business, government, and civil society. In this way, the Institute fosters movements towards more enlightened societies. www.shambhalainstitute.org/about.html

SoL, the Society for Organizational Learning, is an intentional learning community composed of organizations, individuals, and local SoL communities around the world. SoL was created to connect corporations and organizations, researchers and consultants to generate knowledge about and capacity for fundamental innovation and change by engaging in collaborative action inquiry projects. As an action learning community, SoL generates real business and social system results, new intellectual capital and on-going personal and professional networks. www.solonline.org

About the Authors

Mike Green has worked for 25 years as a community organizer to help groups of people come together for collective action. Mike has experience developing neighborhood resident organizations, congregation-based organizations, and community partnerships to address social and economic issues. He was the training director of the Asset Based Community Development (ABCD) Neighborhood Circle; which was a learning organization of over twenty community organizations across North America to learn "what works'" and "what does not work" to use ABCD community organizing. He helped start a small public school in Denver where students, parents, neighbors, teachers, and principal were all partners. Founder of three successful small businesses, Mike is also a licensed clinical social worker and family therapist.

Mike uses his experience to work on two interrelated organizing questions: how can local citizens develop strong community partnerships, and how can agencies effectively support this citizens' development work. His work emphasizes communities getting organized to welcome and include marginalized people as contributing citizens

2745 Julian St., Denver, CO 80211

www.mike-green.org   mikebgreen@mac.com   303-477-2686

Henry Moore was the son of a tobacco sharecropper in rural North Carolina, He graduated from North Carolina A & T State University and earned a master's degree in urban studies from the University of Maryland. He has work in government and community building for more than 30 years.

For 17 years Henry served as assistant city manager of Savannah, GA, where he developed a program to identify and organize resident leaders, promote resident leadership development, and instill community pride. The program materialized in strong partnerships with community-based organizations, neighborhood residents, local financial institutions, and the housing industry. From 1990 through 1997, these partnerships produced nearly 2,000 units of affordable housing and invested over $50 million to improve inner city neighborhoods.

We deep sadness we honor Henry's life and leadership. We miss him. He passed from this world in 2006 - just after showing the cover of this book to his daughter - the front page.

John O'Brien learns about building more just and inclusive communities from people with disabilities, their families, and their allies. He uses what he learns to advise people with disabilities and their families, advocacy groups, service providers, and governments and to spread the news among people interested in change by writing and through workshops. He works in partnership with Connie Lyle O'Brien and a group of friends in 12 countries. He is affiliated with the Center on Human Policy (US). inControl: A National Programme to Change the Organization of Social Care (UK), and the Marsha Forest Centre: Inclusion. Family. Community (Canada).

58 Willowick Dr, Lithonia, GA 30038

www.inclusion.com   johnwobrien@gmail.com